DICTIONARY
SKILLS

KS2

P4 to 7

AUTHORS
Wendy Jolliffe and
Carolyn Jones

EDITOR
Clare Gallaher

ASSISTANT EDITORS
Dulcie Booth and
Roanne Davis

SERIES DESIGNER
Anna Oliwa

DESIGNER
Sarah Rock

ILLUSTRATIONS
Sarah Warburton

COVER ARTWORK
Ian Murray

Text © 2001 Wendy
Jolliffe and Carolyn Jones
© 2001 Scholastic Ltd

Designed using Adobe Pagemaker
Published by Scholastic Ltd, Villiers House, Clarendon
Avenue, Leamington Spa, Warwickshire CV32 5PR

1234567890   1234567890

British Library Cataloguing-in-Publication Data
A catalogue record for this book is available from the
British Library.

ISBN 0-439-01794-7

ACKNOWLEDGEMENTS
Curtis Brown Ltd for the use of an extract from *The Wind in the Willows* by Kenneth Grahame © 1908, The University Chest, Oxford (1908, Methuen); **David Higham Associates** for the use of an extract from *The BFG* by Roald Dahl © 1982, Roald Dahl (1982, Jonathan Cape Ltd); **Oxford University Press** for the use of material from *The Oxford Illustrated Junior Dictionary* compiled by Rosemary Sansome, Dee Reid and Alan Spooner and illustrated by Barry Rowe © 1989, 1996, 2000, OUP (1989, Oxford University Press) and by the same compilers *The Oxford Junior Dictionary* © 1978, 1988, 1995, 2000, OUP (1978, Oxford University Press).

Every effort has been made to trace copyright holders and the publishers apologize for any inadvertent omissions.

The right of Wendy Jolliffe and Carolyn Jones to be identified as the authors of this work has been asserted by them in accordance with the Copyright, Designs and Patents Act 1988.

All rights reserved. This book is sold subject to the condition that it shall not, by way of trade or otherwise, be lent, hired out or otherwise circulated without the publisher's prior consent in any form of binding or cover other than that in which it is published and without a similar condition, including this condition, being imposed upon the subsequent purchaser.

No part of this publication may be reproduced, stored in a retrieval system, or transmitted, in any form or by any means, electronic, mechanical, photocopying, recording or otherwise, without the prior permission of the publisher. This book remains copyright, although permission is granted to copy those pages marked 'Photocopiables' for classroom distribution and use only in the school which has purchased the book, or by the teacher who has purchased the book, and in accordance with the CLA licensing agreement. Photocopying permission is given only for purchasers and not for borrowers of books from any lending service.

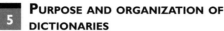

Contents

- **5** Purpose and organization of dictionaries
- **11** Alphabetical skills
- **17** Compiling personal and class dictionaries
- **25** Extending vocabulary
- **37** Definitions and meanings
- **43** Using a range of dictionaries
- **51** Word roots, origins and changes
- **64** Skills grid

Introduction

According to Einstein 'All you need to know is your name, everything else you can look up'. Even if we accept that this remark was rather tongue-in-cheek, it is true that we live in an increasingly information-rich world. There remains the problem, however, of being able to access the information. How many children know that they cannot spell a word, but are unable to use the dictionary that would help them? Even in these days of ICT capability, the same problems persist. A child in a newly acquired class asked me if a word that he had tried to spell was correct. It wasn't. When I suggested that he could check with the electronic dictionary his response was emphatic.

'Yes, but it gives you the wrong word.'

There was an immediate chorus of agreement from the children nearby. Many teachers have had similar experiences with children who get 'the wrong word' from a dictionary. Obviously a dictionary only gives 'the wrong word' when the child concerned does not know how to use it. There is a clear need for a structured and systematic approach to teaching children dictionary skills.

Whether simply looking for a spelling, checking a definition, distinguishing between shades of meaning or seeking further information about the word, children need to know *how* to go about looking for and evaluating such information.

Dictionary skills are a crucial prerequisite if children are going to be able to improve their knowledge of language and ability to write effectively. Research has shown that improving the quality of children's writing is far more difficult than improving the quality of reading. Key skills need to be taught to enable children to develop the independence to write well. This book aims at developing some of these key skills.

Activities in this book will support teaching of word-level objectives, and specific cross-referencing to the National Literacy Strategy framework is provided in the grid on page 64.

The skills developed in this book are:

UNDERSTANDING THE PURPOSE AND ORGANIZATION OF A DICTIONARY

Children need first to be taught about the purpose and organization of a dictionary. They need to be able to find words quickly and efficiently, knowing the quartiles and understanding the purpose of guidewords and headwords, the use of bold type and numbered entries. Specific teaching activities are provided to enable this to be taught.

DEVELOPING ALPHABETICAL SKILLS

Another prerequisite is of course that children have been taught alphabetical skills, ranging from alphabetical order of the first letter of words to second, third and fourth, and so on. A range of activities to enable children to gain experience are provided.

COMPILING PERSONAL AND CLASS DICTIONARIES

As well as being able to find their way effectively around a published dictionary, children need to be able to compile their own dictionaries. This will enable them to have a greater understanding of the structure of a dictionary. In addition, it will greatly enhance their own vocabulary and understanding of a specific area. Constructing their own spelling logs can provide a key means to improving spelling, and activities are included here to develop children's own logs.

EXTENDING VOCABULARY

It is particularly difficult to widen children's vocabulary, especially if they are reluctant readers. This is a key area that dictionary skills can develop. In doing so, they will extend their understanding when reading as well as increasing the range and variety of words used in their writing. Specific activities in this book, covering making collections of new words, exploring homonyms, synonyms, antonyms and metaphors, will enhance children's knowledge and range of words.

INVESTIGATING WORD DEFINITIONS AND MEANINGS

The range of meanings included in dictionaries needs to be demonstrated to children. Activities modelling this are included in this book, as well as some encouraging children to write their own definitions in a concise and effective manner.

USING A WIDE RANGE OF DICTIONARIES

The many different types of dictionaries, including dictionaries of rhyming words, slang, phrases, clichés, synonyms, antonyms, thesauruses and etymology, are explored through a range of activities. These are aimed at helping children understand the functions of the different dictionaries and how to use them for a meaningful purpose. As well as a range in terms of breadth, every classroom needs a range of graded dictionaries to suit all abilities and needs that will enable children to put into practice the skills outlined in this book.

INVESTIGATING WORD ROOTS AND ORIGINS

An understanding of the origins of words, and the effects of adding affixes to root words, can significantly improve children's ability to understand the meanings of words as well as improve their spelling ability. Activities are provided to promote these skills.

INVESTIGATING WORD MEANINGS AND USAGE AND THEIR CHANGE OVER TIME

Enabling children to explore the constantly changing nature of the English language can promote an interest in words that will be reflected in the quality of their writing.

To be an effective writer, to attain the required level at the end of Key Stage 2, requires pupils to develop a range of skills. The activities contained in this book provide a clear means of progression through a number of the necessary skills as set out in the National Literacy Strategy. These are presented in a variety of ways, including games, using a selection of literature to provide a real, meaningful context and, most importantly, to provide the teacher with the means to model the skills required.

PURPOSE AND ORGANIZATION OF DICTIONARIES

The activities in this section focus on children:
- understanding the layout of a dictionary
- knowing how to find their way quickly about a dictionary
- knowing the key purposes of a dictionary, for example spelling and meaning
- knowing that dictionaries contain further helpful information, such as parts of speech.

FINDING YOUR WAY AROUND

RESOURCES AND CLASSROOM ORGANIZATION
You will need: a range of dictionaries (enough for one between two children, if possible); flip chart or board; an enlarged copy of photocopiable page 9 which has had its separate elements cut out plus a copy for each child (for 'Now or later' activities).

Whole-class shared work is followed by independent group work.

WHAT TO DO
Ask the children what a dictionary is used for. (Most children will know that it gives spellings, but some less able children may have only used simple wordbank dictionaries and may be unaware that dictionaries can also give meanings of unfamiliar words.) Ask for volunteers to read out a word from a dictionary for you to try to spell on the flip chart. Ask them to check whether you are right. Then tell the children what you think the word means. This does not have to be exactly what it says in the dictionary! Swap roles with volunteers so that you are reading words out and children are offering spellings or meanings. Continue until all the children are clear about both these two main purposes.

Now hand out dictionaries to the children, and ask them to look at them together. Ask the children what they would say if they wished to explain to someone else what a dictionary page looks like. Start them off by giving an example, such as use of bold type for the headword. Take feedback, listing features on the flip chart to keep for reference. Features you may wish to include are:
- bold type
- use of colour (if any)
- alphabetical order
- the letter of the alphabet as a heading at the start of each section
- the alphabet on every page as a guide (at top/side/bottom)
- headword followed by definition (you do not have to use this terminology)
- spaces between entries so as to tell them apart
- text in columns (some children may not have noticed that they run *down* alphabetically before going to the next column)
- illustrations to clarify the text
- two guide words, one positioned at the top left of the page and one postioned on the top right, which give the range of words on the page, for example *add* to *blink*.

Remove your list and place it to one side where it can be seen.

DIFFERENTIATION
For less able children, use a photocopy of a very simple dictionary page which you have read through with them prior to the lesson. Alternatively make a simple dictionary page with only a few key words, for example *bed, boy, dog, jump, tree*, set out in the same way as the dictionary. More able children can use more advanced dictionaries.

OBJECTIVE
To help children to: understand the purpose and organization of a dictionary.

CROSS-CURRICULAR LINKS
ICT
Using ICT to explore and solve problems.

Now or later

■ Use the cut-out sections from an enlarged copy of photocopiable page 9 to isolate the elements that you listed on the flip chart in the activity (for example the alphabet, the guide words *add* and *blink*, the headwords, for example *ant*, *baby*). Do not show the original page to the children (photocopiable page 9) but show them the jumbled dictionary 'pieces', cut out from the copy of the sheet. Place them randomly on a nearby surface so that they can be seen easily. Refer back to the flip-chart list of how a dictionary page is organized and ask the children to help you create a dictionary page on the flip chart, using Blu-Tack affixed to the back of each piece. You may need to support them in getting the entries in the correct order, as alphabet skills are not the focus of this exercise. They may wish to use a highlighter pen to provide colour for the headwords.

■ In independent group work, children could be provided with a copy of photocopiable page 9 to annotate according to the features on the flip chart.

■ Allow children to take turns to browse through dictionaries on CD-ROMs. Give them five minutes to explore freely, getting used to the CD-ROM, then ask them to compare the CD-ROM version with a page from a class dictionary. Ask them if it is organized in the same way. (It will be, although the definitions will vary slightly.)

How many quartiles in a whole?

Objective
To help children to: know the quartiles of the dictionary.

Cross-curricular links
ICT
Using ICT equipment and software to organize and reorganize information alphabetically.

Resources and classroom organization
You will need: alphabet cards; a range of dictionaries (enough for one between two children, if possible); four small cards marked *first, second, third* and *fourth*; four strips of cards (quartile strips) with letters grouped as follows: **a** b c d; **e** f g h i j k l; **m** n o p q r; **s** t u v w x y z; flip chart or board; Blu-Tack.

Whole-class work is followed by independent work.

What to do
Tell the children that you are going to look for the word *zebra* in the dictionary. Make a great play of looking through the dictionary from the beginning of the *a* section and take a long time. Establish that there are quicker ways of finding words. Explain that the dictionary is divided into sections to make it easier to search for words, and that these sections are known as 'quartiles.' Explain that quartiles are similar to the separate drawers in a chest of drawers for storing different items. (Extend the analogy if you wish by pointing out that just as they would not look for socks in a jumper drawer, it is not helpful looking for the word *zebra* in the *a* section of the dictionary.)

Affix the quartile strips to the flip chart in a line, with a small gap between each one. Read through them with the children, referring to them as the *first* quartile, *second* quartile and so on. Place the *first, second, third* and *fourth* cards above each strip on the flip chart as you do so.

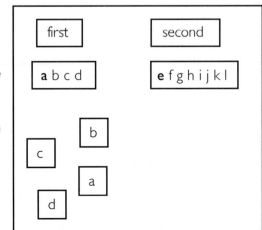

Practise locating letters in the quartiles by using the alphabet cards. Hold up a letter card and ask the children in which quartile it appears. Put each card under the relevant quartile on the flip chart.

Draw attention to the letters in bold, which start each quartile. A useful mnemonic to remember them is **a**lmost **e**very **m**ouse **s**queaks, or the children may prefer to invent their own.

Now tell the children that you are going to try to open the dictionary at these letters – that is, *a, e, m* and *s*). With a little practice and careful judging of the page edges it is possible to open the dictionary halfway to find the *m* section. The children are usually impressed if you can do this at one go! Allow the children to try this for themselves to see how few attempts they can take to find the *m* section. Once they can do this fairly efficiently, move on to show them how to find the start of the second quartile *(e)*, either by judging where a quarter of the pages falls, or by finding a page halfway through, and then dividing again. Similarly, to find the start of the fourth quartile *(s)*, either find the halfway point and divide the rest of the pages in half, or try to gauge three-quarters of the way through. (It is a good idea to have a range of dictionaries to do this so that the children realize that this applies to all dictionaries.)

Now allow the children to work in pairs to practise finding the quartiles.

DIFFERENTIATION

For less able children, use shorter, simpler dictionaries and reinforce the idea of '*m* for middle'. Make sure this is secure before searching for e or s. Once more able children can find *a, e, m* and *s* quickly, see if they can find the 'next' letters – *b, f, n* and *t*, and so on. When they have finished, they could be challenged to use the dictionary to investigate which initial letter is the most common in the English language. (It is *s*, and they do not need to count the words – estimating and checking the pages will do!)

NOW OR LATER

■ Tell the children that they are going to see how knowing the quartiles speeds up looking for words in the dictionary. Put the quartile strips back up on the flip chart and give out the dictionaries. Revise finding the quartile marks. Move on to simple words on cards, asking the children in which quartile they would find the word. Ask the children in pairs to turn to the start of the quartile and encourage them to scan forwards to find the target word. If the word on the card is *cat*, they need the first quartile, so they turn to the *a* section and scan quickly forward to find the c section.

■ Allow children to work in pairs to type a list of words into a simple table and use the sort facility to reorganize it alphabetically.

■ Once they are confident, give the children a list of ten words and challenge them against the clock to see how quickly they can write a 1, 2, 3 or 4 to indicate the quartile and then the page number once they have found the word. Leave the quartile strips visible. Make the choice of words fairly simple for the children initially so that the habit of using the quartiles is established.

word	starts with	which is in quartile	page number	dictionary
mouse	m	3	129	*Oxford Junior*
zebra	z	4	228	*Oxford Illustrated*

Section 1

FIND OUT ALL ABOUT IT

OBJECTIVE
To help children to: understand that dictionaries carry further information about words.

CROSS-CURRICULAR LINKS
ICT
Using ICT to explore and solve problems.

RESOURCES AND CLASSROOM ORGANIZATION
Make an enlarged copy of the sample dictionary page on photocopiable page 9 (or copy it onto an acetate for use with an overhead projector). You will also need a range of dictionaries differentiated to suit the needs of the children. Make enough copies of photocopiable page 10 for one each for the children (for 'Now or later' activity).

Whole-class work is followed by independent group work.

WHAT TO DO
Remind the children that dictionaries can tell you how to spell a word and often will also explain what it means. Tell them that dictionaries can also contain further information about words. Show the children the enlarged dictionary page (photocopiable page 9) and read down through the bold headwords. Ask the children what it says in italic after some of the headwords. (Refer them to work on parts of speech that they will have already covered. Revise definitions briefly if necessary.) Point out that when they look up a word in a dictionary, they will often find out what kind of word it is, as well as its meaning and spelling. Call out words, asking the children to tell you if they are nouns, verbs or adjectives.

Now ask the children to concentrate on the nouns, and explain that in some dictionaries the plural form is given. Remind the children that not all words simply add an s. See if the children can spot nouns on the page which form the plural differently. Point out *bark*, which does not have a plural form.

Ask the children to look for the verbs. Discuss the extra information after the word *verb*. Explain that other forms of the verbs are given. Point out how the *-ing* form is useful for spelling, and that the *-ed* form is the past tense.

Now ask the children to look for the adjectives. Discuss the extra information. Explain that sometimes 'stronger' versions of the adjective are given, for example *bigger* and *biggest*.

DIFFERENTIATION
Read the noun headwords on photocopiable page 9 with less able children before the activity. Ask more able children to use dictionaries to find irregular forms of: nouns (such as those without a plural); verbs (*fights, fighting, fought*, for example); adjectives (such as *good, better, best*). When looking at adjectives, encourage them to notice words which do not have a comparative or superlative form that can be written as a single word, such as *foolish* (*more foolish, most foolish*).

NOW OR LATER
■ Hand out dictionaries to pairs of children. Write a simple word, for example *cake*, on the flip chart and ask the children to look it up and tell you whether it is a noun, verb or adjective. (You could point out that dictionaries can also tell you about other types of words but that you are only concentrating on these for the moment.) Ask what other information is given about the words. Look for sentences or phrases to illustrate the word as well as the definition, or a guide to pronunciation. Ask the children with different dictionaries to compare the information they find.

■ Repeat the exercise above with a list of words that the children are likely to have in their dictionaries, for example *cabin, sad, quack, data…* Ensure that you include a variety of nouns, verbs and adjectives.

■ Ask the children to fill in a copy of photocopiable page 10, in response to a survey of the class dictionaries. Explain that their task is to see what sort of information is given in each one. They should write the name of the dictionary in the first box of the column (there are four columns to allow for the examination of four different dictionaries). This activity could also be done at the computer, with the children using dictionaries on CD-ROMs.

a b c d e f g h i j k l m n o p q r s t u v w x y z

add   blink

add *verb* **adds, adding, added**
1 to put something with something else. *You can add sugar to your tea.*
2 to put numbers together to make a bigger number. *If you add 2 and 2 you get 4.*

address *noun* **addresses**
the details of where a person lives that you put on a letter.

alligator *noun* **alligators**
a kind of crocodile.

angry *adjective* **angrier angriest**
feeling anger. *Mum looked angry so I kept quiet.*
angrily *adverb*

ant *noun* **ants**
a tiny insect. Ants live in large groups called colonies.

baby *noun* **babies**
a very young child.

bacon *noun*
thin slices of meat from a pig.

bad *adjective* **worse, worst**
1 of the kind that people do not want, or do not like. *bad manners, a bad smell.*
2 serious. *a bad accident.*
badly *adverb* *Are you badly hurt?*

bar *noun* **bars**
1 a long piece of wood or metal.
2 a block of chocolate, toffee or soap.
3 a place that serves food and drink at a counter. *a coffee bar.*

bark *noun*
the hard covering round the trunk and branches of a tree.

bark *verb* **barks, barking, barked**
to make the sharp, loud sound a dog makes.

big *adjective* **bigger, biggest**
large, of great size.

blink *verb* **blinks, blinking, blinked**
to close your eyes and open them again very quickly.

Name   Date

Dictionary I spy

■ Write the title of each dictionary across the top, then answer the questions.
■ Add up the columns to find the winner!

	Dictionary 1	Dictionary 2	Dictionary 3	Dictionary 4
Does it tell you what the word means? Score 10 (eg **chat** to talk in a friendly way)				
Does it give you an example sentence? Score 10 (eg **play** he went to the theatre to see a play)				
Does it tell you what sort of a word it is? Score 10 (eg *noun, verb, adjective* or *n, v, adj* for short)				
Does it give you plurals of *nouns*? Score 5 (eg **baby** babies)				
Does it give you any other forms of *verbs*? Score 5 (eg **walk** walks, walking, walked)				
Does it give you 'strengths' of *adjectives*? Score 5 (eg **happy** happier, happiest)				
Does it give you other meanings of the words? Score 5 (eg **cross** 1. To feel annoyed 2. A mark like x or +				
Does it tell you how to say the word? Score 5 (eg **bough** rhymes with cow)				
TOTAL				

Section 2

ALPHABET SKILLS

> The activities in this section focus on children:
> ■ sequencing letters and words in alphabetical order to facilitate access to dictionaries
> ■ developing the confidence to apply their alphabetic knowledge in searching for words in dictionaries
> ■ being able to move quickly through an alphabetically ordered text to locate information
> ■ using their dictionary skills to make their own alphabetically ordered texts.

ALPHABETICAL ORDERING

RESOURCES AND CLASSROOM ORGANIZATION
You will need: alphabet cards (one or two sets, as required); a large alphabet strip for display; a set of simple word cards to sort alphabetically; flip chart or board; Blu-Tack.
Children work as a whole class.

WHAT TO DO
Recite the alphabet with the children, letting them refer to the alphabet strip if they seem to need it. Hand out the alphabet cards, distributing them at random. Explain that each child who has a card is going to hold it up for everyone to see it when their letter is mentioned. Now recite the alphabet again more slowly, with children holding up their letter when it is their turn. Do this in sections, if necessary.

Affix two letter cards to the flip chart with Blu-Tack. Tell the children that they are going to sing through the alphabet to see which of the two letters they get to first. Stop as soon as they get to the first letter. Then reinforce the concept of alphabetical order by identifying the order of the two letters in the alphabet strip. Repeat, stressing the use of running through the alphabet as the means of ordering the two cards.

Ask the children to work in pairs to decide which of their letters comes first in the alphabet. Encourage them to swap cards with another pair. (You may need a second set of cards for this part of the activity.)

Now choose two word cards, for example *pig* and *goat*. Show the matching alphabet cards (*p* and *g*) to the children and ask them which comes first in the alphabet. Explain how the word cards can be put into alphabetical order just by looking at the first letter. Repeat with two new words, linking them to alphabet cards, if needed.

Hand out two word cards to each pair of children and ask them to put them into order, checking with another pair when they have done so. Choose two children to come to the front of the class with their cards, and ask the class which word comes first. Then call more children out one at a time and see if the class can put them into an alphabetical line.

DIFFERENTIATION
For less able children who have problems learning the alphabet, make a tape recording in class of children singing the alphabet. If necessary, record the same sections (*a–g, h–m, n–u, v–z*) several times, with gaps for repetition, before putting the whole alphabet together. Either let the children borrow the tape to take home, or encourage them to listen to it a few times a day in the classroom.

OBJECTIVE
To enable children to: organize words or letters alphabetically, using the first two letters.

CROSS-CURRICULAR LINKS
ICT
Using ICT to explore and solve problems.

GEOGRAPHY
Using and interpreting globes and maps.

For the letter-ordering activity, use only the first section of the alphabet to work within, and have the first section of the alphabet strip available, for the children to use as a guide.

For more able children, allow them to work in fours to order the cards.

NOW OR LATER

■ Hand out the alphabet cards and ask the children to line up in order. Then take every opportunity when children line up to ask them to do so in alphabetical order – by surname/Christian name/girls' names first, then boys' names, and so on. Ask the children to think of a noun and line up alphabetically, for example *ant, bee, cat*…

■ Introduce two new word cards that start with the same letter, for example *tiger* and *tree*. Ask the children how they would put them into alphabetical order. Guide them towards looking at the second letter to see which word comes first. Practise putting a few words that start with the same letter in alphabetical order before handing out word cards (including groups of two words that start with the same letter). Ask the children to work in pairs to put them into alphabetical order, swapping with other pairs as before.

■ As soon as the children can order two words quickly, ask them to join up with other pairs and order four at a time. As a motivator for boys, try using the names of football players (some may have football cards to bring in to sort) or racing drivers.

■ Allow the children to take turns to work in pairs on the computer. Give them up to four word cards and ask them to type them in alphabetical order.

■ See if the children can put names of countries and local place-names into alphabetical order, with a globe and maps on display in the classroom.

■ Play the 'Forwards/backwards' game. Give one pair of children a dictionary. Write the start word on the flip chart, for example *song*. Ask the rest of the class whether the pair with the dictionary should go forwards or backwards to find *sweet/shed/sack* and so on. Have the alphabet strip available for support for those who need it.

ALPHABETICAL SCANNING

OBJECTIVE
To enable children to: scan alphabetical sources.

CROSS-CURRICULAR LINKS
ART
Developing visual perception, selecting and sorting images.

RESOURCES AND CLASSROOM ORGANIZATION
You will need: an enlarged copy of the dictionary page on photocopiable page 16; a set of blank word cards; dictionaries and thesauruses (enough for one between two children, if possible); flip chart or board.

Children work as a whole class initially, then in small groups.

WHAT TO DO
Explain the term 'scanning' to the children. Compare it to how they search for a friend in the playground. You could use an enlarged photocopy of a group photograph to demonstrate the process. Or see if the children are familiar with the 'Where's Wally?' books (published by Walker Books). Draw attention to the way in which they look but don't stop to look closely. Explain that if they want to find a particular piece of information or a word in a dictionary, they can scan in the same way without stopping to read every word closely. Tell the children that they are going to practise scanning texts that are in alphabetical order.

Write a word from the enlarged dictionary page on a piece of card. Read the word

with the class and explain that you are going to play 'Scan snap'. Place the card on the page, over the first word at the top of the first column, then slowly pull the card down the page until you reach the word that matches the word on the card. Do this several times using further cards, each with a different word, stopping at the target word each time and reading the entry.

Next, explain that you are going to do it again but this time you will not write the word for them. Choose another word from the enlarged page, tell the children what it is and scan down the page again to locate it. Use the blank side of a card to move down the dictionary entries, as it will help the children to scan. Remind them that it is important to scan down, rather than in the normal reading direction, to find a word. Repeat, perhaps challenging different groups at a time.

If the children are able to do this well, give out a range of dictionaries and thesauruses. Write a simple word on the flip chart. Remind the children how to use the quartiles of the alphabet to find the start of the section with the first letter. Give the class time to find the start letter, then ask them to begin scanning for the target word.

DIFFERENTIATION

More able children may be encouraged to use the second letter to narrow the area for scanning. Less able children may still need the target word putting on card and having a simpler text from which to work.

NOW OR LATER

■ Ask the children to work in pairs with a dictionary or thesaurus each, and list ten entries from the text. They should then give the list to their partner to add the page number of the dictionary (or thesaurus) where they found each word. Encourage speed.

■ Show the children a picture from the front of a jigsaw box. Then ask one of the children to pick out a jigsaw piece at random from the pieces in the box, and look at it carefully. How quickly can the child scan the picture on the box to find the part which matches the jigsaw piece? This activity is a visual scanning technique which mirrors scanning in reading.

Section 2

DIY ALPHABETICAL BOOKS

OBJECTIVE
To encourage children to: make alphabetically ordered texts.

CROSS-CURRICULAR LINKS
HISTORY
Using dates and terms relating to the passing of time; selecting information relevant to a topic.

GEOGRAPHY
Collecting and recording evidence to answer questions; using appropriate geographical vocabulary.

SCIENCE
Using appropriate scientific vocabulary.

RESOURCES AND CLASSROOM ORGANIZATION
You will need: a flip chart or board; alphabet cards (for 'Now or later' activity).
This is a whole-class introduction to ongoing individual work.

WHAT TO DO
Explain to the children that during the term they are going to make a booklet that will relate to the current class topic (or work to be covered in history/geography/science – whatever subject area you have chosen for the booklet to link with). Explain that it will be alphabetically ordered like a dictionary and look like a mini-encyclopaedia (you may wish to show them an encyclopaedia and read an entry or two). Remind the children of work that they have done on definitions and explain that each entry will have a definition and further details (optional) relating to the entry.

Refer back to the previous term's topic (or the history/geography/science focus). For example, if you were studying the Second World War you might choose *rationing* as an entry and, with the children, devise a short description of what rationing was. Scribe the entry on the flip chart in the style of an encyclopaedia. Explain that this is how you will write all new entries as the term progresses.

These could be typed on the computer, in which case they could be either ordered alphabetically as they are written, or entered one under the other as they arise. You would then print them and ask the children to cut them out and order them manually, as an independent activity. If they are handwritten, you could peg them onto a washing line so that they can be ordered as you go along.

DIFFERENTIATION
For support, give a restricted number of entries for children to order and, if necessary, provide them with very simple definitions that have already been written down.

NOW OR LATER
Make a copy of an index from a poetry book or an information text relating to last term's topic. This can be done by re-keying the text at a computer, printing out the sheet and photocopying it. Now cut up the sheet into separate sections, with each section containing a group of entries for a particular letter, and distribute them to the children. Ask them to lay out the alphabet cards and group the entries under appropriate letter headings.

ALL IN ORDER

OBJECTIVE
To enable children to: use third and fourth place letters to locate and sequence words in alphabetical order.

CROSS-CURRICULAR LINKS
ICT
Using ICT equipment and software to organize and reorganize information.

RESOURCES AND CLASSROOM ORGANIZATION
You will need: a range of dictionaries (enough for one between two children, if possible); a set of blank word cards; flip chart or board; Blu-Tack; individual alphabet strips (for less able children); photocopiable page 16 (for 'Now or later' activity).
Children work as a whole class.

WHAT TO DO
See if the children can still remember how to put two words into alphabetical order (see 'Alphabetical ordering' on page 11). Briefly revise how to sequence words, including words whose first two letters are the same, for example *crisp* and *crack*.

Next write *ink*, *each* and *under* on separate cards, taking care to space the letters evenly. Fix them to the flip chart, one word under the other. Order the words with the children, and then put them to one side of the flip chart but leave them visible and in order.

Now tell the children that you will order some new words. Put up three more cards: *blunder, blink* and *bleach*. Establish with the children that as the first two letters are the same, they will have to look at the third letter to decide which comes first. Hold a blank piece of card over the *bl* to find the third letter of each word, and wait for the children to spot that they have already ordered *ink, each* and *under*!

You can repeat this activity if you wish, using the following shorter and longer words:

Order *idle, and*, then order *bridle, brand*.
Order *eat, urn, art, ill*, then order *cheat, churn, chart, chill*.
Order *etch, anger*, then (by fourth letter) *stretch, stranger*.

Once the children are in the swing of ordering by third or fourth letter you can omit the step in which you have a shorter word within the main word.

Next, write some words on cards and put two words at a time on the flip chart, always lining one up under the other. Use a blank card to mask the start of the word to highlight the letters you will order. Remind the children to run through the alphabet to decide which letter comes first.

Move on to an activity in which the children are asked to locate words rather than sequence them. Ensure that the children have one dictionary between two, and write a target word on the flip chart, explaining that they should try to find the word in their dictionaries. Number over the top of the word in a different colour – that is, put a 1 above the first letter, 2 above the second letter, and so on. Choose a word like *scratch* which has many other words starting with the same string of letters. Make sure that it appears in the range of dictionaries which you have available. Ask the children what the first letter is, and ask them to turn to the start of that section of the dictionary. Ask them to identify the second letter of the word. Get into the habit of asking them whether the letter occurs at the beginning, middle or end of the alphabet, and therefore whether they can expect to find it at the beginning, middle or the end of the *s* section. Ask them to turn to the start of the *sc* section. Repeat for the third letter. When the children are confident in doing this, do not write the target word on the flip chart for them but encourage them to say it aloud and listen to identify the likely letters before beginning to search.

DIFFERENTIATION
Allow less able children access to their own alphabet strip, if necessary. In group work, use familiar vocabulary for them to order. This could be taken from their reading books or spelling work.

NOW OR LATER
■ Play a guessing game. Open the dictionary at random and write the word which appears at the top left of the page on the flip chart. Challenge the children in pairs or groups to see if they can guess any words which might appear on the same page. To extend the activity, repeat but also write the word which appears on the bottom right of the page or double-page spread, and see if the children supply any of the words which lie between them.

■ Play 'Fast find'. Give the children a dictionary between two. Then give them a target word and challenge them to take it in turns to find it in as few 'goes' as possible. Remind them to use the quartiles of the dictionary to find the initial letter (see 'How many quartiles in a whole?' on page 6).
■ Give the children a list of words taken from the sample dictionary page on photocopiable page 16. Ask them to cut out the words and sort them into alphabetical order. When they have finished, give them a copy of the photocopiable sheet to check the order for themselves.

Cc

cab *noun* **cabs**
1 the part of a lorry, bus, or train where the driver sits.
2 a taxi.

cabbage *noun* **cabbages**
a large round vegetable with a lot of green leaves.

cabin *noun* **cabins**
1 a room in a ship or aeroplane.
2 a small hut. *a log cabin.*

cabinet *noun* **cabinets**
a cupboard. *a bathroom cabinet.*
the Cabinet *noun*
the most important people in the government.

cable *noun* **cables**
strong, thick wire or rope.

cackle *verb* **cackles, cackling, cackled**
to laugh and make the sound a hen makes.

cactus *noun* **cacti**
a plant with a thick green stem, covered in prickles. Cacti grow in hot, dry places and do not need much water.

café *noun* **cafés**
a place where you can buy a drink or food.

cage *noun* **cages**
a large box with bars across it for keeping animals or birds in.

cake *noun* **cakes**
a food that you make with flour, fat, eggs, and sugar and bake in the oven.

calamity *noun* **calamities**
something very bad that happens suddenly.

calculator *noun* **calculators**
a machine that can do sums.

calendar *noun* **calendars**
a list showing all the days, weeks, and months in a year.

calf *noun* **calves**
1 a young cow, elephant, or whale.
2 the part of your leg between the knee and the ankle.

call *verb* **calls, calling, called**
1 to speak loudly.
2 to give a name to someone or something. *They called the baby Robert.*
3 to tell someone to come to you. *Mum called us in for tea.*

calm *adjective* **calmer, calmest**
1 still. *a calm sea.*
2 not noisy or excited. *Keep calm. You're safe now.*

calorie *noun* **calories**
a unit used to measure the amount of energy produced by food. If your diet has too many calories, you may put on weight.

camcorder *noun* **camcorders**
a camera for taking video pictures.

came *verb* see **come**

camel *noun* **camels**
a big animal with one or two humps on its back. Camels are used instead of horses in deserts, because they can travel for a long time without eating or drinking.

camera *noun* **cameras**
a machine for taking photographs.

camouflage *verb* **camouflages, camouflaging, camouflaged**
to hide something by making it look like its surroundings.

camp *noun* **camps**
a group of tents or huts where people live for a short time.

camp *verb* **camps, camping, camped**
to make a camp, or stay in a camp. *We went camping last summer.*

definitions from *The Oxford Illustrated Junior Dictionary*, by permission of Oxford University Press

Section 3

COMPILING PERSONAL AND CLASS DICTIONARIES

The activities in this section focus on children:
- developing independent strategies for improving spelling
- keeping a personal spelling log
- compiling a dictionary on a specific theme.

SPELLING WALL

RESOURCES AND CLASSROOM ORGANIZATION
You will need: a copy of the spelling wall on photocopiable page 21 for each child; a piece of work which has a spelling mistake in it (even if it has been corrected) for each child; flip chart or board; writing and colouring materials.

A whole-class introduction is followed by work in pairs.

WHAT TO DO
Ask the children to tell you some of the words that they have trouble spelling. Tell them that you are going to look at an organized way of helping them to learn their own spelling 'hiccups'. Hand out a copy of the spelling wall on photocopiable page 21 to each child. Tell them that this is to be their own personal spelling log where they will collect the words which they need to learn. Ask them to fill in their name and the name of the partner with whom they will be working.

Take one of the words which causes problems, for example *said*, and write it on the flip chart in a commonly misspelled form, such as *sed*. Explain that when you want them to add a word to the spelling wall you will underline the part of the word that they need to learn, and write the correct letter string over the top, for example:

ai
s<u>e</u>d

(You could also use a code such as *sp.w* for 'spelling wall' in the margin.) Take a sample spelling wall sheet and together fill in the word *said*, underlining the *ai*. Explain to the children that when they add a word to their spelling wall they should also underline the part they need to learn.

Give the children time to scan through their own written work to find misspelled words to add to their spelling walls. (You may prefer to have identified spelling mistakes in their work for each of them prior to this session.) Explain that the children should fill in their spelling walls regularly, after their work has been marked or at a specific time you have agreed with them.

Once a week, the spelling walls can be handed out to pairs to take it in turns to test their partners. When a word is spelled correctly a coloured dot should be drawn inside the brick. When a word is spelled correctly three times the whole brick should be lightly shaded in around the word to show that it has been learned. Every now and then the words in the coloured bricks can be tested again. (Parents and carers may like to have a copy of the spelling wall so that they can give support at home.) Collect in the spelling walls regularly to check the spellings. Ask the children to fill each row before starting a new row, so that you can quickly scan new entries for errors.

DIFFERENTIATION
For more able children, increase the number and complexity of the words added to the spelling wall at a time. Allow children who rarely make mistakes to choose words to learn from more advanced dictionaries.

OBJECTIVE
To enable children to:
keep a personal spelling log
to learn previously misspelled words.

Less able children will benefit from the whole-class nature of the spelling-wall routine, a process that will make them feel that they are keeping up with the rest of the class. Ensure that they do not have more than five words to learn at a time and that those on their spelling wall are correctly spelled! Daily two-minute look–cover–write–check practices (every registration session, for example) are very effective.

Now or later
Links with handwriting can be made by asking the children to choose a word from their spelling wall and to practise writing the part of the word (a spelling string, for example, such as *ai*) which they need to learn. They can then practise writing the whole word.

Keeping a log

Objective
To encourage children to: use a spelling log to aid spelling.

Cross-curricular links
English
Checking spellings using wordbanks, dictionaries and spellcheckers.

History
Communicating their knowledge and understanding of history.

Geography
Communicating in ways appropriate to the task and audience.

Resources and classroom organization
You will need: a copy of photocopiable page 22 for each pair (or copy the sheet onto an acetate for use with an overhead projector); an exercise book for each child; writing materials.

Whole-class shared work is followed by independent group work.

What to do
Distribute the exercise books, explaining to the children that these will become their own personalized spelling logs in which they will write words they have misspelled in their work. They will also use them to help them to remember ways of spelling words. (Some children may have already begun to use a spelling log in Years 3 and 4, principally as a personal spelling dictionary.)

Ask the children to write a title on the front cover, 'My Spelling Log', with their name, class and so on, and then to write a contents sheet on the first page, set out as follows:

> **Contents**
> Alphabetical list of words
> Tricky words and how I can remember them
> Spelling rules
> Word families
> Word origins
> Notes

■ **Section 1 Alphabetical list of words:** Now ask the children to complete the first section of their spelling logs. Explain that they should make the alphabetical sections, with the letter of the alphabet written in upper and lower case on the top right-hand corner of the page. Supply the children with a range of words for them to enter. They should place these in the correct alphabetical sections.

■ **Section 2 Tricky words:** Introduce this section when Section 1 has been completed. Begin by discussing 'Ways to remember spellings' on photocopiable page 22. (The answer to the riddle is *mouse*). Offer children plenty of different examples and emphasize that we all have preferred learning styles (visual, auditory or kinaesthetic) – we can choose whatever method works best for us.

Visual methods: draw a picture around the word to emphasize the shape, such as making a boat shape around the word *what*. This helps the word to be remembered because of its simplified form.

Auditory methods: take a commonly used word such as *Wednesday* and say it aloud, deliberately speaking the *d* to remind the children that it is needed when spelling the word. Also, explain how spelling words out letter by letter can reinforce auditory memory, for example p-e-o-p-l-e.

Kinaesthetic methods: colour and trace over a word five times – the more times a word is written down correctly, the easier it will be to remember.

Additional memory tricks: encourage the children to make up their own mnemonics, such as *ight – I go home tonight*. Looking for words within words will help children to examine words closely and remember the correct spelling: *there's a rat in sep**a**rate*.

Ask the children to format each page of this section in the following way:

Words I know	Words to practise	
	Word (underline difficult part)	How I remember it

Use an example of a commonly misspelled word, such as *believe*, to demonstrate how this would be written in the 'words to practise' section, with the part which is often spelled incorrectly underlined. Then you can discuss a way to remember it: 'Never bel<u>ie</u>ve a <u>lie</u>.'

DIFFERENTIATION
As these are individual spelling logs, the words children enter will very much depend on their own level of ability. Encourage children who are struggling with high-frequency words to learn a small number at a time, using the range of strategies set out below.

NOW OR LATER
During subsequent sessions introduce the next parts of the spelling log separately ('Spelling rules' and so on) and provide the children with investigations or activities to carry out which will give them material to add to particular sections. The use of the spelling log will then be an ongoing activity and a constant source of reference. The different sections can be explained to the children as follows:

■ **Section 3 Spelling rules:** Provide one example of a spelling rule, although make it clear to the children that there are nearly always some exceptions. For example: 'When two vowels go walking, the first does the talking; it says its name', such as *goal, boat*.

Encourage the children to build up a number of spelling rules. This may be best achieved by providing them with a range of words to investigate and inviting them to discover the rules themselves, where possible.

■ **Section 4 Word families:** Tell the children that this section will consist of letter strings for them to add to. Point out that this will help them to see that many words in English share the same letter pattern, although not always the same pronunciation. Give them one or two examples to begin the section, for example:

■ **Section 5 Word origins:** Explain that the children should use an etymological dictionary for this section, and that its aim is to encourage them to take an interest in words and their origins. This will help them in understanding meanings of words and in recalling their spelling. (See 'Where does it come from?' on page 45.) Give the children a range of words to investigate, explaining that they should underline the common parts and say what they think the meaning of that part is. They can check by referring to an etymological dictionary or a dictionary that contains information on word derivations. One example might be: *scribble, describe, manuscript, scripture, prescription* (from the Latin *scribere* – 'to write').

MAKING A DICTIONARY

OBJECTIVE
To help children to: compile a dictionary of technical terms.

CROSS-CURRICULAR LINKS
SCIENCE
Using scientific knowledge and understanding to explain observations.

MATHS
Communicating mathematically, including the use of precise mathematical language.

GEOGRAPHY
Using appropriate geographical vocabulary.

ICT
Creating a class database.

RESOURCES AND CLASSROOM ORGANIZATION
You will need: enough copies of photocopiable page 23 for one between two children (or copy the sheet onto an acetate for use with an overhead projector); a copy of photocopiable page 24 for each child (further copies will be required for 'Now or later' activity); a range of science books; dictionaries; writing materials.

Whole-class shared work is followed by independent group work.

WHAT TO DO
Explain to the children that they are going to make their own dictionary and that the finished dictionaries will be combined to make a class dictionary. Show them a copy of photocopiable page 23, which contains a collection of words. Ask them what the words are connected with (science – in particular, forces). Now ask the children to look at the format of the dictionary page on photocopiable page 24 and discuss how the words connected with forces could be organized in a dictionary. Discuss alphabetical order, use of abbreviations and definitions. You will also need to ensure that the children understand the meaning of *guide word* (the words at the top of each dictionary page which give the first and last word on each page) and *headword* (the item in bold which occurs at the beginning of a dictionary entry). Work together with the children to write one or two definitions, for example *upthrust*, meaning 'a force which pushes back up from water, air or a solid surface'.

Now let the children work independently (this could be in groups or pairs) to write a dictionary page of scientific terms on photocopiable page 24. You may like to give groups or pairs different alphabetical sections to cover. Provide a range of scientific textbooks and dictionaries to help them, but ask them to ensure that they write their own definitions. Remind them to put in the guide words when they complete a page. They can add the correct part of speech – adjective, verb and so on – using the abbreviations provided on the photocopiable sheet.

DIFFERENTIATION
Provide the children with the collection of words on forces on photocopiable page 23 to put into alphabetical order. Where possible, they should include a definition for each one. You could also provide some definitions for less able children to match to the correct words.

NOW OR LATER
■ Allow the creation of the dictionary pages to form an ongoing activity over several weeks, with the finished pages being combined to make a class dictionary.
■ Children could use ICT to compile a database of scientific terms, to be included in the class dictionary.

Name   Date

Spelling wall

Ways to remember spellings

■ Decorate or illustrate the word.

■ Find words within words.

■ Create a spelling rhyme for a word.

■ Find six word relations.

■ Carry out a wordsearch in newspapers or magazines for a word.

■ Make words into a crossword puzzle.

■ Write a nonsense sentence including as many particular words being learned as possible.

■ Make a design using the spelling words printed end to end, for example a circle, triangle or spiral.

■ Create a puzzle or riddle, for example:

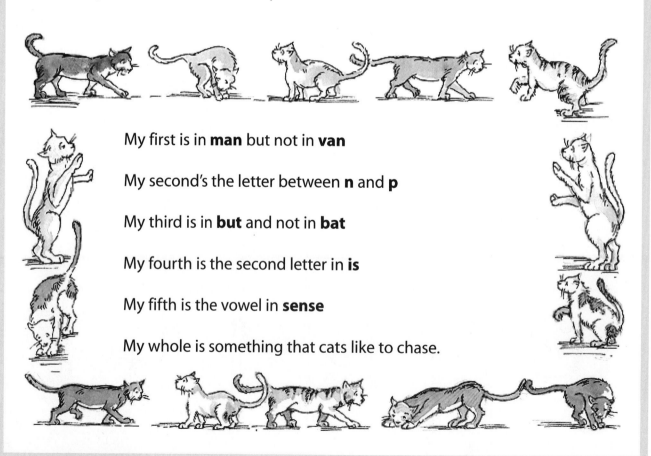

My first is in **man** but not in **van**

My second's the letter between **n** and **p**

My third is in **but** and not in **bat**

My fourth is the second letter in **is**

My fifth is the vowel in **sense**

My whole is something that cats like to chase.

Forceful words

magnetic

repel

attract   force meter

balanced

mass

force

upward force

vibration

friction

gravity   air resistance

upthrust

resistance

surface area

newtons

tension

weight

Name   Date

Dictionary page

Dictionary of _____ terms

Guide word:

Meaning

Word

Guide word:

Meaning

Word

Abbreviations: adj. – adjective; adv. – adverb; conj. – conjunction; n. – noun; pl. – plural; pref. – prefix; prep. – preposition; vb. – verb

Section 4

EXTENDING VOCABULARY

The activities in this section focus on children:
- extending vocabulary
- exploring homonyms
- investigating synonyms
- investigating antonyms
- collecting idioms
- studying metaphors.

COLLECTING WORDS

RESOURCES AND CLASSROOM ORGANIZATION
You will need: an enlarged copy of photocopiable page 32 (or copy the sheet onto an acetate for use with an overhead projector) and individual A4 copies; dictionaries (enough for one between two children); flip chart or board; writing materials.

Whole-class shared work is followed by independent group work.

WHAT TO DO
Explain to the children that they are going to start a collection of new words. You may like to display these as an interesting 'word wall', for example, and children can write the words into their personal dictionaries or spelling logs (see 'Keeping a log' on page 18).

Using the extract from *Alice in Wonderland*, highlight with the children any unusual or unknown words, for example *civil*. Read the sentence which contains the word in question and ask the children to guess what they think the word means. Ask them to think of another word that means the same (a synonym), such as *polite*. Work through several words in the same way – as you do so, point out whether they are nouns or adjectives, and so on.

Distribute copies of the photocopiable sheet and ask the children to work independently, using the extract from *Alice in Wonderland*. Explain that they should underline, or highlight, unknown words, write what they think the words mean, and then check in a dictionary. Write the following format on the flip chart for the children to copy:

Word	My meaning	Dictionary meaning

Finally, play a version of 'Call My Bluff', with one group of children writing words on the board, and providing different meanings, and the rest of the class guessing the real meaning.

DIFFERENTIATION
Provide less able children with a simpler extract of text for them to use, or provide words and meanings on separate cards for them to match.

NOW OR LATER
- Once you have introduced the concept of searching for new and interesting words, this can be an ongoing activity, with new words being regularly added to a class display and children's personal spelling logs.

OBJECTIVE
To encourage children to: collect and categorize new words from reading.

CROSS-CURRICULAR LINKS
SCIENCE
Using their scientific knowledge and understanding to explain observations.

MATHS
Communicating mathematically, including the use of precise mathematical language.

GEOGRAPHY
Using appropriate geographical language.

- Categorize the final collection of words, for example adjectives to describe characters or settings.
- When using non-fiction books, children can identify unfamiliar words and research the meanings either in a glossary or dictionary. A display of words related to a particular theme can then be made, for example words relating to teeth.

WHICH WITCH IS WHICH?

OBJECTIVE
To help children to: explore homophones and differentiate their meanings.

CROSS-CURRICULAR LINKS
ICT
Use ICT equipment and software to organize and reorganize.

RESOURCES AND CLASSROOM ORGANIZATION
Dictionaries (one between two children, if possible); flip chart or board; paper and writing materials.

Children work as a class initially, then in groups.

WHAT TO DO
Tell the children that they are going to look at words called 'homophones' (one of the two types of homonym). Explain that homophones are different words that sound the same, but mean different things, for example *stares* and *stairs*. Write these two words on the flip chart, pointing out the different spelling. Ask the children if they can think of a sentence for each word. Choose one of the suggested sentences and write it on the flip chart with a gap where the word *stares/stairs* would be. Discuss with the children what is the correct word. Explain that it is sometimes difficult to decide which to write when there are words that sound the same. Show the children how to use the dictionary to check.

See if the children can suggest other words which they sometimes confuse, and list them on the flip chart (*knew/new; there/their/they're* are likely culprits). For each homophone, offer the alternatives in short sentences, for example *knew* as in *I knew you could* and *new* as in *I've got a new bike*. Point to the correct word as you do so.

Now tell them that they are going to play 'Homophone challenge'. Hand out dictionaries, one between two or three children. Call out a word and ask the children to use their dictionaries to find and write down possible words. (They may need prompting as to possible spelling choices.) Give one point for each pair or additional word found. Homophones likely to be found in simple dictionaries are, for example: *brake/break; buy/bye/by; dear/deer; fort/fought; groan/grown; hare/hair; hear/here; hour/our; knot/not; meet/meat; pair/pear; to/two/too; won/one; which/witch; your/you're*.

Follow up in group work by writing some short sentences on the flip chart with a choice of homophones in brackets. Ask the children to choose the appropriate homophone. For example, *Go ____ at the corner (right/write)*. Encourage the children to use their dictionaries to check that they have the correct word.

26

Ready to go! DICTIONARY SKILLS

DIFFERENTIATION

For 'Homophone challenge', give less able children simpler dictionaries and less words to look up, but increase the points for each word found. Write the homophones on a list for them to find, and ask them to note down the page numbers when they find the word.

In the group activity, allow the most able children to work in pairs to choose one of the homophones listed in 'What to do'. They can then write their own phrase or sentence to illustrate each possibility, and swap sentences with another pair of children for them to decide which homophone should fill the gap.

NOW OR LATER

■ Prepare a computer version of the homophone cloze exercise and show the children how to use the cut and paste commands. (If you have the facility, choose 'track changes' from the tools menu.)
■ Compile a class list of homophones, encouraging children to add to it as more are discovered. Encourage them to think of mnemonics to distinguish between them – *a st**air** leads up in the **air***, and so on.
■ Make a quiz for children using pairs of homophones. Write one word and next to it in brackets put the definition of its homophone, for example *hair* (a rabbit-like animal). Children can use a dictionary to find the word which sounds the same as the first word but which means the same as the definition in brackets. (NB. *Spell it Yourself Dictionary* by Oxford University Press is particularly useful for work on homophones.)

SWITCH INTO SYNONYMS

RESOURCES AND CLASSROOM ORGANIZATION

You will need: at least one thesaurus; a copy of photocopiable page 33 for each child; flip chart or board; writing materials.

A class discussion at the beginning of the activity leads into group work.

WHAT TO DO

Write the following words on the flip chart: *beautiful, bad, walked, looked*. Explain to the children that these words can be overused and that they are going to find other words which are similar in meaning but are more interesting. Explain that these are called 'synonyms'.

Write the following sentence on the flip chart: *The little girl looked at her mother*. Now ask the children to suggest words that could replace *looked*. Write some of these on the flip chart.

Show the children a thesaurus and explain that it lists synonyms. Turn to the entry *looked* and read the entries to the children. Put a few on the flip chart, including *stared* and *glanced*.

Underline *stared* and *glanced*. Point out that although both words are synonyms for *looked*, they have slightly different meanings. Discuss with the children how useful it is to have a thesaurus that gives them a choice of words so that they can get exactly the effect they want. Ask them which word they would choose if they wanted a word which meant 'to look quickly', 'to look for a long time', 'to look angrily' and so on. Explain that when they use a thesaurus they might need to check the exact meaning in a dictionary.

OBJECTIVE
To encourage children to: investigate synonyms using a thesaurus.

CROSS-CURRICULAR LINKS
ICT
Using ICT to explore and solve problems; using ICT equipment and software to organize and reorganize information.

Ask the children in small groups to choose either *beautiful*, *bad* or *walked* from the flip chart, then see how many alternatives they can think of between them.

Next, hand out copies of photocopiable page 33 and ask the children to choose one of the words and list some of the synonyms. Discuss any unfamiliar words. Then ask them to write a sentence for each synonym which makes the 'shade' of meaning clear, for example *drink: She **sipped** at it because it was hot. She **gulped** it because she was so thirsty*, and so on.

Now or later

- Ask the children to classify words, for example entries for *walk* could be listed in order of speed, starting with the slowest, or words for *cold* listed in degrees of cold, for example *cool, chilly, nippy, freezing*.
- Play the connotations game: can the children find pleasant/unpleasant entries for *look, talk, take, sit, big, smell, small*? For example for the word *smell*, a 'pleasant' entry would be *scent*; an 'unpleasant' one, *stink*.
- Play 'Synonym whispers', with children working in groups. Give one child from each group a piece of paper with a word written at the top, for example *walk*. The child looks at the word, writes a synonym and folds it over so that only the last word is showing and passes it to the next child in the group who does the same. When all have had a turn, the paper is unfolded and the children can look to see how close in meaning the first and last words are.
- Use a simple word-processing program on a computer to type in a list of words. Ask the children to take turns to use the thesaurus facility on the computer to find and list synonyms.

Differentiation

To extend the group work, challenge the most able children to find synonyms for words like *animal, church* and *colour* in a thesaurus. These have words listed which are not synonyms, but are related in some other way, for example *animal* may have *cat* and *rabbit* listed as species of animal. For less able children, use a very basic thesaurus and help them to locate simple words which are part of their reading vocabulary.

ANTONYMS ARE OPPOSITES

Objectives

To encourage children to:
- investigate antonyms using a thesaurus
- develop vocabulary
- explore, develop and clarify ideas
- discuss possibilities.

Cross-curricular links

ICT
Using ICT to explore and solve problems in the context of work across a variety of subjects.

Drama
Role-play.

Resources and classroom organization

You will need: a flip chart or board; different-coloured marker pens; dictionaries (enough for one between two children, if possible).

Children work as a class, then in groups.

What to do

Introduce the topic by running through some obvious opposites like *up/down, tall/short, black/white* and so on. Tell the children that these are called 'antonyms' as well as 'opposites'.

Explain that you are going to look at some particular types of antonyms – words that are very similar in appearance but opposite in meaning. Write the word *possible* on the flip chart. Ask for a word which means 'not possible' (*impossible*). Write it on the flip chart, using one colour for the prefix, and another for the root word. Repeat with *patient* (*impatient*). Ask the children which bit means 'not' (*im*).

Explain that some words form their opposites by taking the root word like *patient/possible* and prefixing it with *im* to make it negative. A warning! Tell the children that *im* does not always mean *not*. *Imprison* is not opposite to *prison*! Ask them where they should check to make sure. (A dictionary.)

Now ask the children if they can think of any other prefix that can make a word into its antonym, and list one example of each. (If children find this difficult, give them the prefix as a prompt.) For example:

im + mature = *immature*
un + able = *unable*
ir + regular = *irregular*
il + legible = *illegible*
in + correct = *incorrect*
dis + appear = *disappear*

Tell the children that there is a suffix that can also form antonyms: *-less*. Give the example *brainless* and take the children through the process of dropping the *-y* from *brainy*. Do the same for *harmful* and *harmless*. Add one example to the list on the board, with the suffix written in the same colour as the prefixes. Model how to check the meanings of words in the dictionary.

Next, hand out dictionaries to the children and ask them to find a page starting with one of the prefixes above. Meanwhile make three columns on the flip chart, headed *Prefix, Root word, Suffix*.

In column 1 *(Prefix)*, write *im, un, ir, il, in, dis*. In column 2 *(Root word)*, write *appoint, cease, responsible, legal, resistible, worth, do, possible, regular, even, harm, tire, fair, legible, brain, mature, perfect, clue*. Under column 3 *(Suffix)*, write *less*. For example:

Prefix	Root word	Suffix
im	appoint	less

With the children, investigate possible combinations to make words. Discuss the meaning of the root and then the antonym. Model the use of a dictionary to check.

DIFFERENTIATION

Once more able children have found one example for each suffix or prefix, ask them to use more advanced dictionaries to find combinations not possible from the chart. Stress the vocabulary extension aspect.

When carrying out the group work with less able children, make the chart as above, but use only the root word and antonym columns. Put in only the following entries: column 1 *(Prefix) un, dis*; column 2 *(Root word) appear, kind, agree, do, like, even, cover, fair, honest, dress*.

Alternatively, give these children a set of small cards, with one word which is part of an antonym written on each one, and ask them to make pairs and then write the antonyms.

NOW OR LATER

■ Children can take turns to enter antonyms into a document, then run the spellcheck to see which words the computer does not recognize, for example *undiscover*!
■ Ask the children to do some drama work in pairs: explain that they have to mime two antonyms and the rest of the class must guess what they are. If they find this difficult, make an antonym bank from which the children can choose words.
■ Children can make card games based on opposites, for example versions of 'Snap' or 'Pairs'.
■ Ask the children to work in groups on antonyms, completing a table set out as below.

Root word	Meaning	Prefix or suffix	Antonym
clear	easy to understand	un	unclear

Collecting idioms

Objective
To enable children to: collect and classify a range of idioms.

Cross-curricular links
History
Finding out about events, people and changes studied from an appropriate range of sources of information.

Resources and classroom organization
You will need: enough copies of photocopiable page 34 for one between two children (or copy the sheet onto an acetate for use with an overhead projector); dictionaries of idioms (if available) or dictionaries that contain the meanings of idioms (The Wordsworth *Wordmaster Dictionary* by MH Mauser and ND Turton is an excellent and inexpensive source); a copy of photocopiable page 35 for each child; flip chart or board; paper; writing and drawing materials.

Whole-class shared work is followed by independent group work.

What to do
Display the copy of photocopiable page 34, showing sample entries of idioms, or give one copy of the sheet to each pair. Ask the children if they know what an idiom is. Make sure that they know that it is a phrase that is not meant to be taken literally – the overall phrase has a figurative or non-literal meaning. For example, explain that the expression *It's raining cats and dogs* does not mean that cats and dogs are falling down from the sky, just that it is raining very heavily. Look carefully at the sample entries on the photocopiable sheet with the children and discuss how the dictionary has grouped together all the idioms in which the word *make* can be found and then given their non-literal meaning. Ask the children if they can think of any other idioms that are commonly used, and list them on the flip chart.

Now provide the children with the list of idioms on photocopiable page 35 and ask them to write two sentences for each, one with the literal meaning and one with the figurative meaning. They could also provide a humorous cartoon illustration of the figurative meaning.

It was the last straw.

Finally, ask the children to compare their literal and non-literal interpretations of the sentences on photocopiable page 35.

Differentiation
Less able children could concentrate on cartoon drawings of idioms to show their literal meaning.

It was the last straw.

Now or later

■ Play a game in which the children ask each other to guess the idiom by looking at an illustration they have drawn which illustrates the figurative meaning.
■ Make a collection of idioms for display, and include the children's humorous illustrations.

Find the metaphor

Resources and classroom organization

You will need: a range of dictionaries, including dictionaries of idioms or clichés, if possible; a copy of photocopiable page 36 for each child; flip chart or board; writing materials.

Whole-class shared work is followed by independent group work.

What to do

Discuss the meaning of the word *idiom* (see previous activity, 'Collecting idioms'), reminding the children that it is a phrase that cannot be deduced literally, and the word *metaphor* (a phrase in which something is described as if it is something else). Therefore a metaphorical expression or figure of speech is very similar to an idiom, although it may not be so common or well known. Brainstorm a range of metaphorical expressions with the children and write them on the flip chart, for example *He was a fish out of water*, *He had a finger in every pie*.

Now ask the children to read the extract of text on photocopiable page 36, and to underline all the metaphorical expressions. They can then rewrite the text without the metaphors.

Finally, compare the original text on photocopiable page 36 with the rewritten versions. Are the children's versions an improvement or is too much of the meaning lost?

Objective

To enable children to: investigate metaphorical expressions and figures of speech in everyday life.

Differentiation

Less able children could be asked to simply identify the metaphorical expressions on photocopiable page 36 rather than being given the additional task of rewriting the text. Encourage more able children to use a range of dictionaries to check on meanings when they are working on the photocopiable sheet.

Now or later

■ Ask the children to write their own stories containing metaphorical expressions.
■ Compile a list of metaphors, as an ongoing activity, to be added to in the classroom.

A mad tea party

There was a table set out under a tree in front of the house, and the March Hare and the Hatter were having tea at it. A Dormouse was sitting between them, fast asleep. The table was a large one, but the three were all crowded together at one corner of it. "No room! No room!" they cried out when they saw Alice coming.

"There's plenty of room," said Alice indignantly, and she sat down in a large armchair at one corner of the table.

"Have some wine," the March Hare said in an encouraging tone.

Alice looked round the table, but there was nothing on it but tea. "I don't see any wine," she remarked.

"There isn't any," said the March Hare.

"Then it wasn't very civil of you to offer it," said Alice angrily.

"It wasn't very civil of you to sit down without being invited," said the March Hare.

"I didn't know it was *your* table," said Alice. "It's laid for a great many more than three."

"Your hair wants cutting," said the Hatter. He had been looking at Alice for some time with great curiosity, and this was his first speech.

"You should learn not to make personal remarks," Alice said, with some severity. "It's very rude."

The Hatter opened his eyes very wide on hearing this; but all he said was, "Why is a raven like a writing-desk?"

"Come, we shall have some fun now!" thought Alice, "I'm glad they've begun asking riddles – I believe I can guess that," she added aloud.

"Do you mean you think you can find the answer for it?" asked the March Hare.

"Exactly so," said Alice.

"Then you should say what you mean," the March Hare went on.

"I do," Alice hastily replied. "At least – at least I mean what I say – that's the same thing, you know."

"Not the same thing a bit!" said the Hatter. "Why, you might just as well say that 'I see what I eat' is the same thing as 'I eat what I see'!"

"You might just as well say," added the March Hare, "that 'I like what I get' is the same thing as 'I get what I like'!"

from *Alice's Adventures in Wonderland* by Lewis Carroll

Thesaurus page

bad	1. *a bad man:* beastly, cruel, malevolent, mean, naughty, wicked, vile 2. *a bad accident:* appalling, awful, dreadful, ghastly, hideous, nasty, serious, terrible 3. *bad work:* appalling, faulty, feeble, pitiful, poor, useless, weak
beautiful	appealing, artistic, attractive, brilliant, charming, dainty, elegant, exquisite, fascinating, glamorous, graceful, handsome, lovely, magnificent, neat, picturesque, pretty, quaint, scenic, spectacular, superb
big	1. *a big amount:* ample, bulky, considerable, enormous, extensive, fat, grand, great, huge, hulking, large, lofty, massive, monstrous, spacious, terrific, vast 2. *a big decision:* grave, important, major, serious, significant
cold	1. *cold weather:* Arctic, biting, bitter, bleak, chill, chilly, cool, freezing, frosty, frozen, icy, nippy *(informal)*, perishing, raw, wintry 2. *cold feelings:* callous, cool, cruel, hard, hard-hearted, unfeeling, unfriendly
drink	to gulp, to guzzle, to lap, to sip, to swallow, to swig *(informal)*
look	to behold, to contemplate, to examine, to eye, to gaze, to glance, to glare, to glimpse, to peep, to peer, to scan, to see, to squint, to stare, to study, to view, to watch
nice	The word *nice* has many meanings. For some of the other words you can use see *beautiful, good, pleasant*
sit	to be seated, to perch, to rest, to squat
small	1. *a small baby:* diminutive, little, minute, tiny 2. *a small book:* brief, compact, short 3. *a small TV:* portable, miniature 4. *small helpings:* meagre, measly, microscopic 5. *a small problem:* insignificant, minor
smell	aroma, fragrance, incense, perfume, reek, scent, stench, stink *(informal)*, whiff
take	1. *take my hand:* clutch, grab, grasp, hold, seize, snatch 2. *the soldiers took prisoners:* to arrest, to capture, to corner, to seize 3. *Who took my pen?* to move, to remove, to nick *(informal)*, to pinch *(informal)*
talk	to babble, to bawl, to blurt out, to chat, to chatter, to cry, to drone, to gabble, to gossip, to harp, to jabber, to lisp, to mumble, to mutter, to prattle, to rave, to recite, to screech, to snarl, to splutter, to spout *(informal)*, to stammer, to stutter, to whisper
walk	to amble, to crawl, to creep, to hike, to hobble, to limp, to march, to pace, to paddle, to plod, to prowl, to ramble, to saunter, to shuffle, to slink, to step, to stride, to stroll, to stumble, to trek, to trot, to trudge, to waddle
wash	to bath, to bathe, to clean, to mop, to rinse, to shampoo, to sponge down, to swill, to wipe

Idioms

The word **make** features in many idiomatic expressions, including:

make ends meet to be able to balance how much money you have with how much you spend. It originated from 'ends' being the ends of the year and the money you had at the beginning of the year lasted until the end.

make hay while the sun shines to take action while conditions are favourable, taken from when a farmer cut his grass while the weather was dry.

make no bones about it speak plainly about something and take direct action. It probably came from bones in soup, so if there were no bones, it would be easier to eat.

makes one's blood boil something makes you very angry. It probably came from the 17th century, although if the temperature of blood reached boiling point, a person would be dead.

make or break to go into something knowing that you will either succeed or fail. It is used by Charles Dickens in *Barnaby Rudge*.

make your hair stand on end a frightening experience; comes from the Bible (Job 4) and refers to the goose pimples that come on when someone is scared or startled.

make the grade come up to the required standard – from the American railroad locomotive which had to do this to climb a hill.

make your mouth water a strong desire for something; is likened to dogs salivating at the sight of food.

Take it literally

■ Write two sentences for each idiom, one to show what it means literally and the other to show what is really meant by the idiom. You can use a dictionary to help you.

1. To beat about the bush.

2. To kill two birds with one stone.

3. To get to the bottom of.

4. To cut a long story short.

5. It's not the end of the world.

6. It was the last straw.

7. She is a pain in the neck.

8. To pay through the nose.

9. To pick holes in someone.

10. To pull one's socks up.

11. To rub it in.

In plain English

■ Underline the metaphorical expressions and rewrite the passage in plain English.

John first saw the light of day in a tiny cottage in a remote part of the country. From that day to this he was always a fish out of water whenever he entered the big city. But the day came when he had to bring home the bacon and even though he was all at sea, he put his back into it and went full steam ahead.

As the years went by he felt he had been led down the garden path and he had the wool pulled over his eyes. A friend finally let the cat out of the bag and he decided to get to the bottom of it. In the end he had to let sleeping dogs lie and he retired to his cottage in the country just a shadow of his former self. He eventually pulled himself together and lived a simple but contented life. He decided never to return to the city in a month of Sundays.

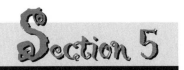

Section 5

DEFINITIONS AND MEANINGS

The activities in this section focus on children:
- understanding that one of the main purposes of a dictionary is to clarify meaning
- realizing that a word may have more than one meaning and using a dictionary to identify the appropriate definition
- developing the ability to write dictionary style definitions of their own with increasing economy and clarity.

MULTIPLE MEANINGS

RESOURCES AND CLASSROOM ORGANIZATION
You will need: dictionaries (enough for one each for a group of children); enlarged format dictionary; flip chart or board; paper and writing materials.

Whole-class shared work is followed by work in groups or pairs.

WHAT TO DO
Discuss with the children how we find out about word meanings, and examine examples of dictionaries. Now using an enlarged format dictionary, look at the word *line*. Talk about the print features such as bold type and its purpose to highlight specific words. Read the definitions, discussing the use of numbered definitions. Write the word *line* on the flip chart, in the middle of the paper, and make a semantic web of all the possible meanings:

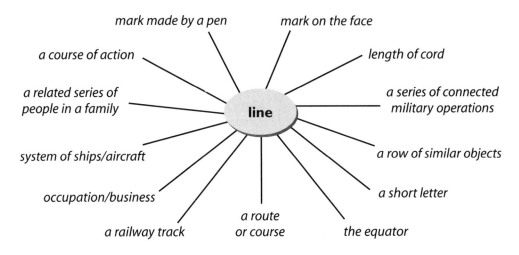

Now provide the children with several words to investigate, such as *table, green, note, level, field, drive*, by writing them on the flip chart and asking the children to draw their own webs showing different word definitions (using a dictionary). Encourage them to give feedback to the rest of the class, when they have completed the activity.

DIFFERENTIATION
Provide the children with a range of dictionaries according to their ability.

NOW OR LATER
- Enlarged semantic webs can be displayed in the classroom as an aid to vocabulary extension.
- Challenge the children to find the word with the most possible definitions.

OBJECTIVE
To help children to: understand that dictionaries include different definitions of a word.

Section 5

OBJECTIVES
To encourage children to:
- use dictionaries to learn or check the definitions of words
- use the term 'definition'.

CROSS-CURRICULAR LINKS
ART
Experimenting with ideas for their work suggested by visual and other source material.

ICT
Using a computer to print out information; using ICT equipment and software to communicate ideas and information, incorporating text and pictures.

SCIENCE AND GEOGRAPHY
Using appropriate vocabulary.

TRUE OR FALSE?

RESOURCES AND CLASSROOM ORGANIZATION
You will need: a range of dictionaries (enough for one between two children, if possible); an enlarged copy of photocopiable page 9 with small Post-it Notes over the definitions for *alligator, ant* and *blink*, leaving the words themselves visible; small cards with *T* on one side, *F* on the other.

Children work as a whole class, then in groups.

WHAT TO DO
Ask the children to tell you the two main uses of a dictionary (for spellings and the meanings of words). Tell them that you are going to concentrate on the meanings in dictionaries and that the other word for the meaning is the *definition*. Use the two terms interchangeably from now on. Display the enlarged copy of photocopiable page 9. First read the definitions for *baby, bacon* and *bar* with the children. Discuss whether each definition fits in with the children's understanding of the word. Now look at *alligator, ant* and *blink*. See if the children can guess what the hidden definitions are, and explain that different dictionaries might have slightly different definitions.

Now play the 'True or false?' game, distributing the small cards with *T* and *F* on them, one to each child. Choose an easily definable word such as *bonfire* from the dictionary and read out either the correct definition or an adjacent definition of another word. Ask the children to indicate whether it is true or false by holding up their cards to show *T* or *F*. After the class has 'voted', ask a child to read out the definition in the dictionary to check the meaning. Then ask for volunteers to take over from you.

Allow the children to work with one dictionary in groups of two or three to play the 'True or false?' game, taking turns to read or vote.

DIFFERENTIATION
Extend this activity by allowing children to use more advanced dictionaries and encouraging them to select more demanding or specialized vocabulary, such as terms currently in use in geography or science. Less able children could play the 'True or false?' game by matching a limited selection of picture and word cards.

NOW OR LATER
- Let the children play a small group game in which one player reads a definition from a dictionary and the other players guess the original word, then swap round.
- Children could design posters that require the reader to match up words and their definitions. These could be designed using a drawing/writing package on a computer.
- Make a selection of cards with words on one side and definitions on the other. (These could be keyed in at a computer, then printed, cut out and pasted onto cards.) Include some that are not correct. Explain that children have to sort them into true and false piles. Ensure that dictionaries are available for them to make checks.

Ready to go! DICTIONARY SKILLS

Devious definitions

Resources and classroom organization
You will need: a range of dictionaries; flip chart or board.
Children work as a class, then in pairs within small groups.

What to do
Ask for someone to tell you what a definition is. Tell the children that you are going to work on making up definitions. Demonstrate the process orally, using objects from around the room, for example *a window is… a space in the wall, covered in glass to let in light*. Do several, making it quick and fun. Ask for volunteers to take over from you, allowing several children to have a go. Ask children to try this in pairs, taking turns. Then take over again, this time explaining that you will now do the same with verbs ('doing words'). Use familiar action verbs like *sit, look, walk* and so on. Repeat the process of allowing the children to have a go.

Moving on to group work, choose a short list of words (use only nouns and verbs at this stage and avoid words with multiple meanings) from a range of dictionaries in your class. List them on the flip chart, on separate sheets under the heading of the dictionary you wish the group to use, for example:

Blue group (easiest) eg *A First Dictionary*	**Green group** (middle) eg *Weetabix Dictionary*	**Red group** (hardest) eg *Oxford Junior Dictionary*
cake a food made with flour, butter, eggs and sugar	robot	rink
mumps	look	medallist

Ask the children to read the word, discuss with a partner what they think it means, then look it up in the dictionary to check before writing out the definition, as shown above for *cake*.

Next, ask the children to sit with someone from a different group. Ask each child to share with a partner one of the words which he or she looked up. This could be done by playing the 'True or false?' game (see the previous activity), if wished.

Differentiation
During the group work, encourage more able children to use vocabulary from other curricular areas, for example *circuit* (science). You may wish them to use the glossary of a textbook to check their definitions. Prepare a sheet of words for the less able children to define, based on their reading vocabulary. Include the page numbers of the dictionary in which they are found.

Now or later
■ Leave a selection of dictionaries and cards, with a word written on each one, on display. Ask the children to define the word before looking it up in a dictionary to check the meaning. Allow them to work in pairs, one child to think of a definition for the word on the card, the other to look in the dictionary to check the meaning, offering hints if necessary. Invite the children to leave their own words for others to look up.
■ Play the 'Riddle-me-ree' game. Divide the class into two teams. Each team takes it in turn to define a familiar object. Either team can answer. The first team to do so correctly scores ten points; twenty points for words linked to scientific or geographical vocabulary, for example; five points lost for identifying a wrong answer.

Objective
To encourage children to: define familiar vocabulary in their own words.

Cross-curricular links
Maths
Developing oral and mental calculation strategies.

THE DEFINITION DASH

Section 5

OBJECTIVES
To enable children to:
- write their own definitions of words.
- develop their speaking and listening skills, discussing possibilities.

CROSS-CURRICULAR LINKS
PSHE
Developing the cognitive skills of reflecting and evaluating.

RESOURCES AND CLASSROOM ORGANIZATION
You will need: mini whiteboards (enough for one between two children) or a supply of A4 scrap paper; writing materials; dictionaries (enough for one between two, if possible).

Children work as a class and in pairs.

WHAT TO DO
Refer the children back to the work on definitions they have already done (see the previous activity). Ask someone to remind you what a definition is. Explain that in this session they will concentrate on writing their own definitions.

Hand out a mini whiteboard and pen, one between two, or scrap paper to the children. Ask them to work in pairs to write a definition for the word *bucket*, for example (explain that their writing should be large enough for the rest of the class to read easily). When each pair has written their definition, ask them to hold it up for everyone to read; encourage the children to compare the definitions. Discuss which is the best and why. Allow a member of the class to use the dictionary to read out the definition, again for comparison purposes. Repeat the process with several different words.

Now play the game 'Definition dash'. Divide the class into two halves, teams A and B. Each team should appoint a 'decoder', who moves to the opposite side of the room to maintain eye contact with his or her own team and stands further back, behind you.

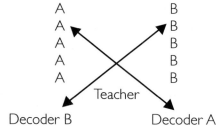

Write a word on a piece of paper or a mini whiteboard and hold it up for both teams to see it, but out of sight of the decoder. Each pair in the team must write a definition as quickly as possible on the whiteboard or piece of scrap paper and hold it up for their own decoder to see.

The first decoder to guess the word on your card wins five points for their team and swaps places with another person from their team.

DIFFERENTIATION
If necessary, have the children in ability groups during the first class activity, and give less able groups easier objects to define – it will help them if they have had time earlier in the day to prepare their responses. During the 'Definition dash' game, ensure that children work in mixed-ability pairs to provide support for each other.

NOW OR LATER
- Play a history or geography version of 'Definition dash'.
- Play 'Definition snap': either the same word or its definition counts as a match.
- Ask the children to produce a list of definitions of local slang, for example *croggy* means 'a lift on a bike'.
- Ask children to write kennings, a type of poetry in which objects are defined by what they do, for example a window would be *a light letter, a rain stopper, a wall spacer*. A dictionary could be used to give ideas. Display the finished kennings without a title so that the object has to be deduced by its description.
- Children could list proverbs and write definitions for them.
- Play the following game, with children working in teams of three or four. Each team

chooses an unfamiliar word from the dictionary and writes it on a piece of card. Its definition is written on the other side of the card. Two nonsense words are made up with accompanying nonsense definitions and written on either side of cards. Each team can then either guess which is the correct definition (for ten points) or look up a word in the dictionary (but then only win five points). If the answer is still wrong, no points are won. The other team then takes a turn.

Short and snappy definitions

Resources and classroom organization
You will need: a copy of photocopiable page 42 for each child; mini whiteboards (enough for one between two children) or a supply of A4 scrap paper; writing materials; a range of dictionaries; flip chart or board.

Children work as a whole class, then in groups.

What to do
Either briefly recap work already done on definitions, or introduce the idea that a definition is the meaning of something, and read one or two from a dictionary. Make up a few for the playground or other area within the school environment such as *the hall – a large room for meeting or exercise; the kitchen – a room for cooking food*.

Once the children have grasped the idea orally, move on to quick written definitions on the whiteboards or scrap paper. Allow the children to discuss what to put and to show each other their definitions once they have written them. Write one of the longer suggestions on the flip chart and discuss how to make it as short as you can. Carry on defining familiar objects as succinctly as possible. Ask for a definition of, for example, *stepladders* in no more than ten words, then ask the children to rewrite the definition in, say, five words or fewer. Always ask them to hold up their versions to show each other. Compare them with the entries in several different dictionaries.

Allow the children to take turns to write their definitions on a computer. As they shorten them, ensure that they use 'track changes' from the tools menu, or copy and paste the original before changing it so that they can see 'before' and 'after' versions.

Move on to group work, handing out copies of the crossword on photocopiable page 42. Tell the children that the answers are already there but they need to write the clues. Explain that writing the definition of the word in the crossword should provide a perfect clue to the word. Some of the vocabulary may be unfamiliar to the children and so will provide another opportunity to use their dictionaries. When the children have finished, encourage them to compare their clues. They can then take turns to write their definitions on a computer.

Differentiation
During the class work, give less able groups simpler objects for definition and if necessary do not restrict the number of words. Challenge more able children to write even shorter definitions. For the group work allow less able children access to a dictionary for any words which they have difficulty in defining, and let them use a dictionary to check the meanings of unfamiliar words when they are writing definitions for the crossword on the photocopiable sheet.

Now or later
■ Challenge more able children to work in pairs to make up a simple crossword on squared paper, leaving the answers in but omitting the clues. Let them swap with another group of children to provide the clues, or leave the crossword on display. The crosswords could be laminated, with wipe-off pens being provided.
■ Play 'definition' team games, each side challenging their opponents to define a word in as few words as possible. The challenger must have a short version prepared. Act as referee to decide if the definitions offered are clear enough.

Objective
To encourage children to: write a concise definition within a given number of words, expressing themselves confidently and clearly, using the conventions of discussion.

Cross-curricular links
ICT
Using ICT equipment to organize and reorganize information; using equipment for a variety of purposes including word processing.

PSHE
Practising co-operative skills in a team situation; learning skills for following instructions.

What's the clue?

				¹b	e	l	l	o	²w			³m	
	⁴s	t	a	r	e				a			i	
	a			d					i			s	
	d		⁵l	u	r	c	h		⁶l	i	n	e	
				a								r	
				g			⁷a	c	r	o	b	a	t
		⁸f	u	d	g	e						b	
				l		⁹g						l	
	¹⁰w	h	i	n	e		a		¹¹g			e	
	h				¹²d	r	i	z	z	l	e		
	i						e		a				
	¹³s	o	¹⁴g	g	y			¹⁵n	a	¹⁶s	t	y	
	p		r					c		a			
	e		o	¹⁷r	a	¹⁸t	t	l	e		d		
	r		w			e				¹⁹d	i	n	
			l			a					l		
				²⁰h	a	m	m	e	r		e		

Across

1
4
5
6
7
8
10
12
13
15
17
19
20

Down

1
2
3
4
9
10
11
14
16
18

Section 6

USING A RANGE OF DICTIONARIES

The activities in this section focus on children:
- using rhyming dictionaries
- exploring a range of dictionaries
- understanding and using etymological dictionaries.

RHYMING DICTIONARIES

RESOURCES AND CLASSROOM ORGANIZATION
You will need: rhyming dictionaries (such as the *Penguin Rhyming Dictionary* and *Pelican Rhyming Dictionary* by R Ferguson); a copy of photocopiable page 47 for each pair (or copy the sheet onto an acetate for use with an overhead projector); writing materials.

Whole-class work is followed by independent group work.

WHAT TO DO
Begin by telling the children that if they want to find a particular rhyme in a rhyming dictionary they will first need to look in the index. This will provide a number that shows them where to find the rhyme. Look at the sample rhyming dictionary page together on photocopiable page 47. Discuss the words that can be found and explain that they all share the same sound but not the same spelling. Talk about the differences in the length of words (the number of syllables) and how more obscure words have definitions in brackets. If you have access to a rhyming dictionary Big Book (such as the *Pelican Rhyming Dictionary*), you can model finding several different rhyming words. Note that the format of this dictionary is much simpler and not numbered. You may also wish to ask different children to find rhyming words in a smaller dictionary and describe how they do so to the class. Talk about the possible uses of this dictionary, one of the main ones being for writing poetry.

Now ask the children to write a simple jingle or limerick using the sample rhyming page on the photocopiable sheet or rhyming dictionaries, if you have sufficient. You could provide an opening line to help them get started, for example *There was an old woman from Hull…*

DIFFERENTIATION
Help less able children to write limericks by providing them with text to complete, for example:

There once was a lady from the Isle of Wight
Who woke up one day with a terrible _____
She opened one eye
And gave an almighty _____
As a monster loomed right into _____

There once was a woman from Surrey
Who went home in a terrible _____

There was an old man from Kent
Whose knees were awfully _____

Encourage more able children to experiment with writing other types of rhyming poems, for example a clerihew – a four-line verse with two rhyming couplets.

OBJECTIVE
To enable children to:
use a rhyming dictionary.

CROSS-CURRICULAR LINKS
ICT
Making a database of rhyming words.

Now or later

Compile some rhyming wordbanks, to display alongside the children's poems in the classroom, for example:

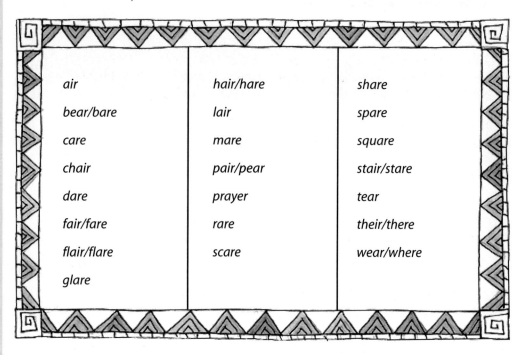

air	hair/hare	share
bear/bare	lair	spare
care	mare	square
chair	pair/pear	stair/stare
dare	prayer	tear
fair/fare	rare	their/there
flair/flare	scare	wear/where
glare		

Using a range of dictionaries

Objective
To encourage children to: investigate and understand the purposes of a range of dictionaries.

Cross-curricular links
Maths
Communicating mathematically, including the use of precise mathematical vocabulary.

Science
Using their scientific knowledge and understanding to explain observations.

Resources and classroom organization
You will need: a wide range of dictionaries; a copy of photocopiable page 48 for each child; flip chart or board; writing materials.

Whole-class shared work is followed by independent group work.

What to do
Show the children as wide a range of dictionaries as possible, for example dictionaries of slang, phrases, idioms, clichés, synonyms, antonyms, quotations, proverbs, maths. Write joint definitions of the terms 'idiom', 'synonym', 'antonym', 'proverb' and 'cliché' on the flip chart and discuss with the children when they might use each type of dictionary. (See also the activities on investigating antonyms, idioms and metaphorical expressions on pages 28, 30 and 31.)

Definitions of terms

Idiom   a phrase which is not meant literally, and its meaning cannot be gleaned from the meaning of each individual word.

Cliché   a phrase which has become overworked over time.

Synonym   a word which has the same or very similar meaning.

Antonym   a word with an opposite meaning.

Proverb   a saying which has changed little over time and uses an idea to teach something.

Now ask the children to match the entries to the correct dictionary on photocopiable page 48.

Finally, encourage the children to discuss their answers to the photocopiable sheet. Display the definitions of terms in the classroom for future use.

Differentiation
Limit the number of entries (and range of dictionaries) that less able children have to match, for example provide them with a mathematical dictionary and mathematical terms, and a dictionary of phrase and fable and a list of titles of fables.

Now or later
Provide children with opportunities to use different types of dictionaries, for example give them a list of proverbs and ask them to look up the meanings in a dictionary of proverbs.

Where does it come from?

Resources and classroom organization
You will need: etymological dictionaries (the *Concise Dictionary of English Etymology* by Walter W Skeat, published by Wordsworth Editions is an inexpensive example); an enlarged copy of photocopiable page 49 and one copy per pair of photocopiable page 50 (or copy the sheets onto acetates for use with an overhead projector); flip chart or board; paper and writing materials.

Whole-class shared work is followed by independent group work.

What to do
If the children are not familiar with the function of an etymological dictionary, show them an example and explain that *etymological* means 'the origins and development of words'. Explain that all words have a story behind them and most of our words come from either Old English language, Norse that the Vikings spoke, or French that came to English with William the Conqueror. Some words go back to Latin or Greek and today words continue to come into our language from other countries. Most good dictionaries contain information on the origin of words, but in order to learn more detail an etymological dictionary is needed.

At this point, give the children an example to illustrate the discussion, for instance, explain that in Roman times each Roman soldier was given an allowance to pay for the salt he needed to preserve food. The Latin word for salt is *sal*. Today there is an English word meaning 'wages paid by the month or year'. Ask the children if they know what it is. *(Salary.)*

Now show the children the sample entries from an etymological dictionary on photocopiable page 49. Ensure that they understand the entries by discussing them together. Explain that there are a lot of abbreviations and that it is

Objective
To help children to: understand the function of an etymological dictionary and use it to study words of interest and significance.

Cross-curricular links
History
Finding out about events, people and changes studied from an appropriate range of sources of information.

Geography
Describing where places are.

important to know what these mean. A list of the abbreviations is contained at the front of most etymological dictionaries. Show a sample of this (photocopiable page 50) on the overhead projector or provide copies of the sheet.

Now ask the children to work independently to find out information about the following words. Provide etymological dictionaries if possible (for more able children) or alternatively, many dictionaries, such as *The Oxford Primary School Dictionary* will provide information about word origins.

List the words in the left-hand column of the table below on the flip chart. Provide the answers for the first word *(sherbert)*, then ask the children to fill in the rest of the table (answers are in italics).

English word	Language of origin	Old word	Old meaning
sherbert	Arabic	sharabat	drink
caravan	*Persian*	*karwan*	*convoy*
yoghurt	*Turkish*	*yogurt*	*food prepared from milk*
sofa	*Arabic*	*suffat, suffah*	*to put a seat to a saddle*
dessert	*Latin*	*de + servire*	*to serve*
shampoo	*Hindustani*	*champna*	*to join, press, thrust in, kneading or pressure*
alligator	*Spanish*	*el largarto*	*the great lizard*
adder	*Old English*	*naedre*	*snake*
denim	*French*	*de nimes*	*from Nîmes in France*
umbrella	*Italian*	*ombrella*	*parasol*
ketchup	*Malay/Chinese*	*kechap*	*fish sauce*

Discuss the children's findings at the end of the activity.

DIFFERENTIATION

More able children could work with etymological dictionaries, with the less able working with simpler dictionaries which provide information on word origins.

NOW OR LATER

Investigations into word origins could be an ongoing activity and form part of work children do independently in their spelling logs (see 'Keeping a log' on page 18).

A rhyming dictionary entry

372 –ite

bite	krait *(venomous snake)*	highlight
byte *(computer term)*	fright	twilight
kite	sprite	headlight
fight	sight	sidelight
height	site	floodlight
light	tight	limelight
blight	Wight	sunlight
flight	white	moonlight
plight		flashlight
sleight	frostbite	spotlight
slight	cordite *(an explosive)*	termite
might	graphite	midnight
mite	ophite *(type of rock)*	good-night
smite	dogfight	fortnight
knight	bullfight	playwright
night	gunfight	typewrite
spite	prizefight	upright
quite	starlight	eyesight
right	daylight	campsite
write	perlite *(volcanic rock)*	airtight
bright	skylight	skintight

Name   Date

Which dictionary?

■ Choose the correct type of dictionary for each entry.

phrase and fable   **antonym**   **cliché**
                idiom
mathematical   **synonym**   **proverb**

Entry	Type of dictionary
at cross purposes misunderstanding each other.	
Those who live in glass houses shouldn't throw stones. Don't speak ill of others unless you are faultless yourself.	
gone to the dogs decline, come to a bad end.	
stale – fresh	
fat – chubby	
parallel Lines are parallel if they never meet, no matter how far they are extended.	
lion's share the largest or best part; all or most. Originates from one of Aesop's fables in which several animals joined a lion in a hunt. When they were dividing the spoils, the lion claimed one quarter as his right, one for his courage and one for his mate and cubs. He challenged the animals to argue with him for the last quarter, but they were too intimidated and left.	

Etymological dictionary entries

Atlas (Gk.)
Named after Atlas, the demi-god who was said to bear the world on his shoulders; his figure used often to appear on the title-page of maps, now known as atlases.

Barracks (F. Ital.)
F. *baraque*, Ital. *baracca*, a tent for soldiers.

Bayonet (F.)
bayonnette – a knife, named from Bayonne in France where first made.

Bungalow (Pers. – Bengalee)
a Bengal thatched house, from the name Bengal.

Chocolate (Span. – Mexican)
cacao – from the Mexican name of the fruit of the tree from which chocolate is made.

Melody (F. L. Gk.)
Gk. a song, ode.

Meteor (F. Gk.)
raised above the earth, soaring in air, anything suspended.

Potato (Span.)
patata, a potato.

Tuxedo (U.S.)
a dinner jacket first worn at The Tuxedo Park Country Club near Tuxedo Lake in New York State. Tuxedo derives from P'tuksit, the name given to the region around Tuxedo Lake by its previous Indian inhabitants. This means 'the one with a round foot' or 'wolf'.

definitions 1-8 from *The Concise Dictionary of English Etymology*, by permission of Wordsworth Editions Ltd

Common abbreviations

Arab.	–	Arabic
A.S.	–	Anglo Saxon
C.	–	Celtic
Corn.	–	Cornish
Dan.	–	Danish
Du.	–	Dutch
E.	–	Modern English
M.E.	–	Middle English
F.	–	French
O.F.	–	Old French
Gael.	–	Gaelic
G.	–	German
Gk.	–	Greek
Heb.	–	Hebrew
Hind.	–	Hindustani
Icel.	–	Icelandic
Ital.	–	Italian
L.	–	Latin
Norw.	–	Norwegian
Pers.	–	Persian
Port.	–	Portuguese
Russ.	–	Russian
Scand.	–	Scandinavian
Span.	–	Spanish
Swed.	–	Swedish
Turk.	–	Turkish
U.S.	–	USA
W.	–	Welsh

Word roots, origins and changes

The activities in this section focus on children:
- collecting and classifying word roots
- identifying roots of words
- inventing words using word roots
- exploring word origins
- understanding the evolution of words.

Collecting words with common roots

Resources and classroom organization
Make an enlarged copy of photocopiable page 57 (or copy the sheet onto an acetate for use with an overhead projector). You will also need: a copy of photocopiable page 58 for each child; one dictionary per pair; a class etymological dictionary; flip chart or board and different-coloured marker pens; writing materials.
Whole-class shared work is followed by independent group work.

What to do
Share the extract from *The Wind in the Willows* on photocopiable page 57 with the whole class. Read the text with the children and ensure everyone understands the content. Now highlight the word *visible* and explain that there are other words which use the letters *vis* in this word to form other words. Write the following words on the flip chart, using two colours:

visible
vision
in**vis**ible
tele**vis**ion
visit
visionary
visitor
visitation
re**vis**ion

Talk about the letters that are the same each time and ask the children if they can guess what the letters *vis* mean. You can then either tell them that *vis/vid* means 'to see' from the Latin, or use an etymological dictionary to research the meaning. Now provide pairs of children with a dictionary and ask them to look up the meaning of each word in the list above. You could make it a race against time for each word, awarding points to the quickest pair.
Repeat the process, using the word *spectactor* (the plural *spectators* is in the extract). This time list the following:

spectator
in**spec**t
spectacles
su**spec**t

Again ask the children to look up the meanings and discuss a common meaning (*spec* – 'to see' from Latin).
In independent group work, children can sort words from photocopiable page 58

Objective
To help children to: collect and classify words with common roots.

Cross-curricular links
History
Finding out about events, people and changes studied from an appropriate range of sources of information.

into common roots, finding meanings in a dictionary and working out the meaning of the root word.

> **Answers to 'Sorting common word roots' on photocopiable page 58**
>
> mob – to move tract – to pull
> port – to carry mar – sea
> cap – head   sens – feel

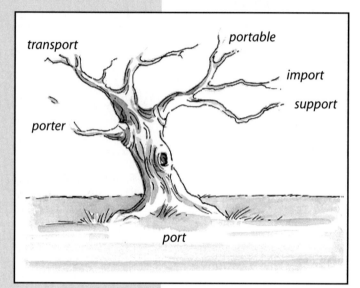

At the end of the activity, encourage the children to share meanings of the root words that they have found.

Differentiation
Give more able children further extracts of text (possibly from *The Wind in the Willows*) to scan to find words with common roots. Make sure that less able children are given fewer words to sort, with words provided on card and letter patterns highlighted.

Now or later
Results of investigations of word roots could be displayed on a wall poster which highlights in different colours common word roots.

Find the word root

Objective
To enable children to: identify word roots, derivations and spelling patterns.

Cross-curricular links
Science
Investigating words related to science topics.

History
Linking with derivations of words related to a particular topic.

Resources and classroom organization
Copy the word roots and derivations on photocopiable page 59 onto card, and laminate and cut out the individual cards. You will also need: dictionaries (enough for one between two children, if possible); etymological dictionaries; flip chart or board; Blu-Tack; paper and writing materials.

Whole-class shared work is followed by independent group work.

What to do
Choose two examples from the word root cards (printed in bold) and fix them onto the flip chart with Blu-Tack, for the children to see, for example *form* and *science*. Scatter some examples of derivations around the two root words and select children to match the root words with derivations, for example:

form   **science**
uniform   conscience
formation   conscious
transform   scientific
formula

Brainstorm as many other derivations of the root words and write them on the flip chart. Discuss the meanings of these and ask different children to check them in the dictionary. Using an etymological dictionary, check the meaning of the root (*form* – 'shape' from Latin; *sci* – 'know' from Latin).

Now write the list of root words below onto the flip chart and ask the children to work independently to find as many possible derivations as they can. Do not give the meanings at this stage, but ask the children to try to find them out. Provide dictionaries for support.

Root word	Meaning
struct	build
man	hand
act	do
multi	many
tex	weave
loc	place
sign	mark
temp	time
var	different
rupt	break
geo	earth
phon	sound

Finally, encourage the children to share their examples of derivations, writing them as word webs on the flip chart.

DIFFERENTIATION
Provide less able children with the root cards and derivations and explain that they can play a card game. Each child starts with four root cards and then takes it in turn to select a word from the derivation cards which are placed in a pile in the centre. If the derivation matches the root, the player may keep it. The first person to collect four derivations for each of the roots is the winner.

NOW OR LATER
Display word webs, with word roots and derivations, in the classroom. Place word cards of roots and derivations next to the display for children to sort as an ongoing activity.

LANGUAGE EXCHANGE

RESOURCES AND CLASSROOM ORGANIZATION
You will need: a copy of photocopiable page 60 for each pair (or copy the sheet onto an acetate for use with an overhead projector); a range of dictionaries showing word derivations; an etymological dictionary; flip chart or board.

Children work as a whole class and then in groups.

WHAT TO DO
Look carefully at photocopiable page 60 together, which shows some Greek words and their translations. Now write on the board the following words:

acrobat	crocodile	astronaut	thermometer
telephone	octopus	hippopotamus	autobiography
megaphone	geography	archbishop	microcomputer
antiseptic			

OBJECTIVE
To enable children to: identify everyday words developed from another language.

CROSS-CURRICULAR LINKS
HISTORY
Finding out about events, people and changes studied from an appropriate range of sources of information.

Refer back to the photocopiable sheet and now take one word as an example, say, *crocodile* (meaning 'gravel worm' – from the Greek *kroke* – 'gravel' and *drilos* – 'worm'). Ask the children if they can identify any similar Greek words to crocodile. You may like to provide some guidance for this first attempt. Write a joint Greek translation on the flip chart, set out as follows:

kroke + *drilos* = *crocodile*
(gravel) (worm)

Now work through one or two other examples together until the children are familiar with identifying the Greek translation.

Ask the children to continue working through words you have put on the flip chart, setting it out as above.

DIFFERENTIATION
For less able children, draw lines to show links on page 60 before photocopying it, for example:

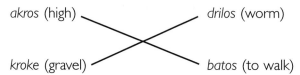

NOW OR LATER
■ Ask the children to identify where the following words (which you have either put on the flip chart or on a separate sheet) have come from, using their dictionaries:

algebra	biro	hospital	judo	kebab	macho
magazine	malice	perfume	pizza	shampoo	vodka

■ Display a world map and encourage the children to label it with word cards and pieces of string pointing to countries from which the words originated. Add to it as the term goes on.

SPLIT AND SPELL THE WORD

OBJECTIVE
To enable children to: use word roots, prefixes and suffixes as a support for spelling.

RESOURCES AND CLASSROOM ORGANIZATION
You will need: a range of dictionaries including etymological ones; a copy of photocopiable page 61 for each child; flip chart or board; scrap paper/small whiteboards; writing materials.

Children work as a whole class, then independently in groups.

WHAT TO DO
Remind the children of previous work they have done on investigating roots of words and explain that you are going to develop this to split words into roots, prefixes and suffixes, using knowledge of the meanings and how to spell these parts of the words to spell more difficult words. Give some examples, such as *aquamarine* and *aquaplane*.

Now explain that you are going to split the words up into prefixes, roots and suffixes. In the case of *aquamarine*, say that you are going to split it into *aqua* and *marine*. Brainstorm as many words as possible that begin with *aqua* (*aqualung, aquarium, aquatic*) and ask the children what they think *aqua* means – you could also ask a child to look it up in an etymological dictionary ('water'). Now ask someone to look up *marine* (a word relating to the sea) and decide on a definition for the whole word. Write the correct spelling on the flip chart and talk about how knowledge of the different parts helps with spelling the word and working out its meaning.

In independent work, provide children with copies of photocopiable page 61, which is a list of words for them to split into prefixes, roots and suffixes. They should then work out the meaning of each word.

At the end of the activity, ask the children to spell the following words, either by writing on scrap paper or using small whiteboards and pens:

concede   agoraphobia   binoculars

Write the correct spelling of each word on the flip chart and split the words into their prefixes, roots and suffixes. Discuss the meaning of the root words:

con – with   cede – to yield or give up
agora – market place   phobia – fear
bi – two   oculus – eye

Differentiation
Select suitable words – the more common ones – for less able children from photocopiable page 61, such as *bicycle* and *microphone*. Provide similar words for them to work with, for example *biceps, telephone*...

More able children can investigate further words with the same roots.

Now or later
Compile a class glossary of root words and their meanings and derivations.

Make up a word

Resources and classroom organization
Photocopy page 62 onto an acetate for display with an overhead projector, or make an enlarged photocopy of the sheet. Make a list of word roots, prefixes and suffixes from which children can make up words, for example: *micro, scope, photo, graph, con, clude, trans, port, re, sign, ex, port* and so on (put them in jumbled order). You will also need: dictionaries (also etymological ones); flip chart or board; writing materials.

Whole-class shared work is followed by independent group work.

What to do
Begin by reading the extract from *The BFG* by Roald Dahl on photocopiable page 62, which many children will be familiar with. Highlight all the made-up words and talk about whether parts of them are real words. For example, in the word *murderful* the word that can be found is *murder*. Ask the children what word would normally be used (*murdering*). Look for other examples in the text.

Now refer to previous work on word roots, prefixes and suffixes and list some on the flip chart, for example:

aero – air   pre – before
aqua – water   re – again
phone – sound   clude – shut
phobia – fear   scope – look
super – greater   sub – under
port – carry   con – together

Objective
To encourage children to: invent words using known roots.

Cross-curricular links
Science
Investigating the meaning of root words which link with science work.

History
Exploring words which link to a particular topic, for example in work on the Romans finding the derivation of words from the Latin.

Ask the children to suggest made-up words using the roots, prefixes and/or suffixes, for example *aquaphone, aerophobia*, and discuss their possible meanings.

For independent group work, give the children the list of word roots, prefixes and suffixes that you have prepared and ask them to make up as many words as possible, then to add the meanings, checking in a dictionary if necessary.

DIFFERENTIATION

Let less able children work with root words and prefixes on cards to make up words. More able children could check the derivation and meanings of word roots in an etymological dictionary.

NOW OR LATER

Compile a collection of nonsense words used in *The BFG*. These can then be used in a classroom display which shows the giant's words in speech bubbles.

CHANGING WORDS

OBJECTIVE
To encourage children to: understand that vocabulary changes over time.

CROSS-CURRICULAR LINKS
HISTORY
Finding out about events, people and changes studied from an appropriate range of sources.

RESOURCES AND CLASSROOM ORGANIZATION

Photocopy page 63 onto an acetate for display with an overhead projector, or make an enlarged photocopy of the sheet. You will also need: a range of dictionaries; extracts from classic texts, re-keyed; flip chart or board; writing materials.

Whole-class shared work is followed by independent group work.

WHAT TO DO

Following a shared reading of the extract from *Little Lord Fauntleroy* by Frances Hodgson Burnett on photocopiable page 63, highlight words in the text which are not now commonly used – *carriage, coupé, parlour* and so on. Read the words in context and ask the children to say what they think they might mean. Explain that words are constantly changing, and give an example of a word that has changed recently, for example *wicked*, which now has an additional meaning.

Distribute the extracts from a classic text and ask the children to highlight words that are not now commonly used. Explain that they must then list them and write what they think they mean. Encourage them to check the meanings in a dictionary.

In a plenary session, share meanings of words that have changed over time.

DIFFERENTIATION

Provide less able children with specific words to check the meaning of and ask them to write one or more sentences containing the words.

NOW OR LATER

Continue a study of words changing over time by looking at particular words in extracts from Shakespeare that are no longer used (such as *yonder, thither* and so on). An ideal resource would be *An Introduction to A Midsummer Night's Dream* by Linda Marsh (Pelican Big Books series) in which children could pick out words in Oberon's speech to the sleeping Titania:

What thou seest when thou dost, wake,
Do it for thy true love take
Love and languish for his sake.

Collecting words with common roots

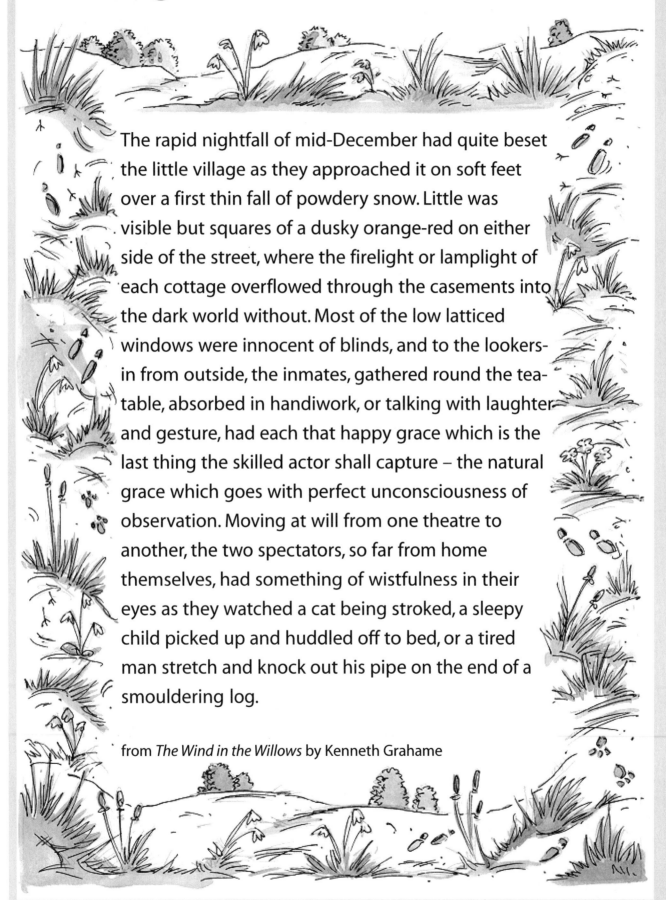

The rapid nightfall of mid-December had quite beset the little village as they approached it on soft feet over a first thin fall of powdery snow. Little was visible but squares of a dusky orange-red on either side of the street, where the firelight or lamplight of each cottage overflowed through the casements into the dark world without. Most of the low latticed windows were innocent of blinds, and to the lookers-in from outside, the inmates, gathered round the tea-table, absorbed in handiwork, or talking with laughter and gesture, had each that happy grace which is the last thing the skilled actor shall capture – the natural grace which goes with perfect unconsciousness of observation. Moving at will from one theatre to another, the two spectators, so far from home themselves, had something of wistfulness in their eyes as they watched a cat being stroked, a sleepy child picked up and huddled off to bed, or a tired man stretch and knock out his pipe on the end of a smouldering log.

from *The Wind in the Willows* by Kenneth Grahame

Sorting common word roots

sensation

mobile

cap

marine

port

captain

mobility

subtract

important

attract

portable

submarine

retract

sense

tractor sensation

immobile

export

porter

import maritime

sensible

transport

capital

mariner

automobile

portmanteau

support

capitulate

decapitate

Word roots and derivations

act	actor	action
react	activity	reaction
flex	flexible	reflex
reflect	deflect	flexibly
miss	missile	mission
transmit	dismiss	missionary
pend	suspend	pendulum
appendix	suspense	pendant
form	uniform	formation
transform	formula	conscience
science	scientific	conscious

It's all Greek to me!

Akros (high)

hippos (horse)

auto (self)

mega (big)

geo (earth)

kroke (gravel)

astron (star)

thermos (heat)

tele (far)

okto (eight)

arch (chief)

micro (little)

anti (against)

drilos (worm)

phone (sound/voice)

metron/meter (measure)

potamus (river)

pous (foot)

batos (to walk)

graph (write)

nautilus (sailor)

bios (life)

■ Can you spot one or two of these Greek words in an English word that you know?

Split and spell the words

Word	Prefix	Root	Suffix	Meaning
biped	bi	ped		bi – two, ped – foot animal with two feet
bicycle				
aquaplane				
aquarium				
microphone				
microscope				
audience				
audible				
transplant				
transport				
autograph				
autobiography				
biology				
geology				

Note:
bi means *two*
audi means *hear*
port means *carry*
aqua means *water*
trans means *across*
auto means *self*
micro means *small*
ology means *study*
graph means *to write*

Made-up words

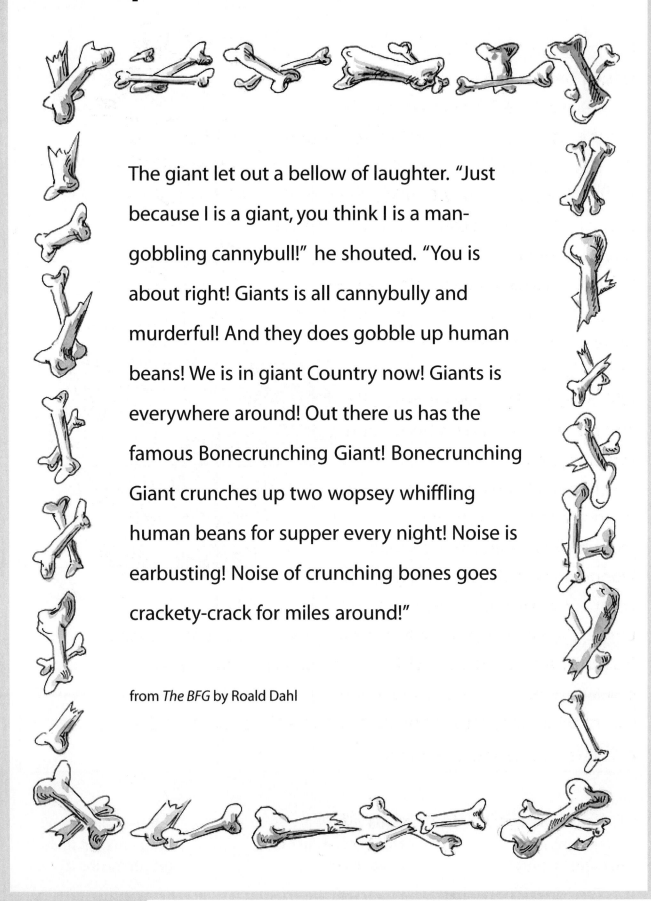

The giant let out a bellow of laughter. "Just because I is a giant, you think I is a man-gobbling cannybull!" he shouted. "You is about right! Giants is all cannybully and murderful! And they does gobble up human beans! We is in giant Country now! Giants is everywhere around! Out there us has the famous Bonecrunching Giant! Bonecrunching Giant crunches up two wopsey whiffling human beans for supper every night! Noise is earbusting! Noise of crunching bones goes crackety-crack for miles around!"

from *The BFG* by Roald Dahl

Little Lord Fauntleroy

Mr Havisham drew his head in at the window of his coupé and leaned back with a dry smile.

"Bravo, Lord Fauntleroy!" he said.

As his carriage stopped before the door of Mrs Errol's house, the victor and the vanquished were coming towards it, attended by the clamouring crew. Cedric walked by Billy Williams and was speaking to him. His elated little face was very red, his curls clung to his hot, moist forehead, his hands were in his pockets.

…That morning Mr Havisham had quite a long conversation with the winner of the race – a conversation which made him smile his dry smile, and rub his chin with his bony hand several times.

Mrs Errol had been called out the parlour, and the lawyer and Cedric were left together. At first Mr Havisham wondered what he should say to his small companion. He had an idea that perhaps it would be best to say several things which might prepare Cedric for meeting his grandfather, and perhaps for the great change that was to come to him. He could see that Cedric had not the least idea of the sort of thing he was to see when he reached England, or of the sort of home that waited for him there.

from *Little Lord Fauntleroy* by Frances Hodgson Burnett

NATIONAL STANDARDS FOR KEY SKILLS

All of the activities listed are designed to extend children's vocabulary and spelling skills through developing their ability to work with a range of dictionaries effectively.

Title	Key skills	NLS objectives
Section 1 Finding your way around How many quartiles in a whole? Find out all about it	Understanding the purpose and organisation of a dictionary Knowing the quartiles of the dictionary Understanding that dictionaries contain further information about words	Y3 T1 W15 Y3 T2 W22 Y3 T3 W15
Section 2 Alphabetical ordering Alphabetical scanning DIY alphabetical books All in order	Organizing words or letters alphabetically, using the first two letters Scanning alphabetical sources Making alphabetically organized texts Using 3rd and 4th place letters to locate and sequence words in alphabetical order	Y3 T2 W23 Y3 T3 T17 Y3 T3 T24 Y4 T1 W12
Section 3 Spelling wall Keeping a log Making a dictionary	Keeping a personal spelling log to help to learn misspelled words Developing the use of a spelling log to aid spelling Compiling a class or group dictionary	Y3 W5, Y4 W2 Y5 W1, Y6 W1 Y5 T2 W9, Y5 T3 W13
Section 4 Collecting words Which witch is which? Switch into synonyms Antonyms are opposites Collecting idioms Find the metaphor	Collecting and categorizing new words from reading Exploring homonyms and differentiating their meanings Investigating synonyms using a thesaurus Investigating antonyms Collecting and classifying a range of idioms Investigating metaphorical expressions	Y3 T1 W13, Y3 T2 W17 Y3 T3 W12 Y3 T3 W14 Y5 T1 W7 Y5 T2 W10 Y5 T1 W9 Y5 T2 W12
Section 5 Multiple meanings True or false? Devious definitions The definition dash Short and snappy definitions	Understanding that dictionaries contain multiple meanings of words Using dictionaries to check the definitions of words Writing own definitions of words Defining familiar vocabulary in their own words Writing a concise definition within a given number of words	Y3 T3 W15 Y3 T2 W19 & 21 Y3 T2 W20 Y4 T1 W11 Y4 T2 W12
Section 6 Rhyming dictionaries Using a range of dictionaries Where does it come from?	Using a rhyming dictionary Investigating and using a range of dictionaries Using an etymological dictionary	Y4 T1 W13 Y5 T3 W11 Y6 T1 W10
Section 7 Collecting words with common roots Find the word root Language exchange Split and spell the word Make up a word Changing words	Collecting and classifying words with common roots Identifying word roots, derivations and spelling patterns Identifying everyday words borrowed from other languages Using word roots as a support for spelling Inventing words using known roots Understanding that vocabulary changes over time	Y4 T3 W7 Y5 T1 W8 Y5 T3 W8 Y6 T1 W5 Y6 T3 W5 Y4 T2 W11, Y6 T1 W7 Y6 T2 W7